IN SYSTEM

THE EYES ARE THE SAME

SUSAN GOLD

Full Court Press
Englewood Cliffs, New Jersey

First Edition

Copyright © 2007 by Susan Gold

Published in the United States of America by Full Court Press, 601 Palisade Avenue, Englewood Cliffs, NJ 07632.
www.fcpress.com

Editing and Book Design by Barry Sheinkopf
Colophon by Liz Sedlack
Author Photograph by Barry Sheinkopf

OCT - 1 2007

FOR LIZA, JONATHAN, AND THEIR FAMILIES,
That the past my heart remembers should not become a myth.

"We struggle to achieve all that we want to achieve—namely, that origins should not be our destiny."

—*John le Carré*

Acknowledgements

The strength and tenacity to complete this memoir were encouraged by many friends in useful ways, including my associates at the Hidden Child Foundation in New York City, and I appreciate all their efforts.

The most vital and steadfast editorial assistance and guidance came from Barry Sheinkopf, Director of The Writing Center in Englewood Cliffs, New Jersey. I am also deeply grateful to my dear friend and colleague Alex Motyl for reading this memoir, for his invaluable editorial help and assistance with historical and geopolitical problems of the old Hapsburg Austro-Hungarian Empire, and for perfect transliterations.

Equally as important was the support of Dr. Paul Dince, who encouraged, crystallized, and worked with me to transform my "non-remembrance" into a literate work of memory, history, and, hopefully, a special legacy for the Holocaust.

Finally, many thanks to Albert Flecha, whose work and computer savvy helped me cut and paste and punch the keys on the word processor, and to my friend Dr. Jamie Rubin, whose very frequent emergency stops regarding the computer's dysfunction were both invaluable and empowering to push on in mysterious cyberspace.

Illustrations---The Eyes Are the Same

FOREWORD
ON MEMORY

MUCH HAS BEEN SAID about voluntary and involuntary memory in literature. How to write about my childhood? How to stop remembered experiences from "slipping away" from children and grandchildren? My Jewish identity and tenuous Polish roots resonate with the wounds of the Shoah.

Antoni Slonimski once described the Poles and Jews as "the saddest two nations on earth, tragically entangled." When the Germans invaded and occupied Poland, we found ourselves outside the circle of compassion. The Nazi destruction of the world I knew, and the primitive hostility of Poles and Ukrainians, left a permanent mark on me. I don't think an outsider can fully understand this condition.

Such events inflict boundless fear and horror on a child. Even today, I viscerally remember that world. How is one to resolve these fears, have a productive life, and believe in human values, justice, and creativity? When we came to America, I fled into the present and visions of a better future, putting thousands of miles between me and what used to be called home and hoping never to see it again.

Yet although I willed my past to be a desert, I could not entirely let go, and I wanted to maintain at least a toehold in the land of my childhood—that quasi-mythic territory between my fifth and thirteenth year. With time, the past was resurrected and returned. Surely lost souls are entitled to be remembered. With an almost subliminal expectation of catastrophe, I eventually permitted an entire ghost city to live in my head and willed myself to remember more and more. Returning to my past self was an occasion for emotion: Certain things endure and have a way of returning unexpectedly, even after a very lengthy absence. Remembering and retracing long-buried recollections, which I had never dared disturb, brought me back to my past childhood, caused endless anxiety, and opened frozen emotions. But my very ambivalence allowed me to dig, breathe, move around, tap into forgotten memories, and describe.

Such remembrances do not proceed as a narrative. I did not want to develop an inner narrative of fantasy with the introspective virtues of hindsight. I have "hunted in the dark" instead and recreated a childhood that, I know, the very process of writing has shaped and distorted. I have tried simply to set down what and how a child innocent of adult self-knowledge saw. Except for the section in Chapter 13 that imagines my cousin Pipa's sudden appearance at a wedding, everything else is as I have remembered experiencing it as a child. I have, in writing about my childhood, used the Polish place names that we then used. Today, Zloczów would be the Ukrainian Zolochiv, Lwów would be L'viv, and Wlodzimierz Wolyñski would be Volodymyr Volyn's'kyy.

I was born in Zloczów, Poland, and lived in Wlodzimierz Wolyñski, the home of my father's family. Wlodzimierz, a town of about 20,000 in the Pripyat' region, was first mentioned in chronicles in the tenth century. It was a fortified trading town, second only to Kiev in importance as a seat of the Eastern Church. The first Jewish settlement of Wlodzimierz goes back to the twelfth century, when Tatar-Mongol raids led the presumed descendants of the Khazars, a

Turkish tribe that converted to Judaism in the eighth century, to migrate West. In the eighteenth century, when Poland was partitioned, Wlodzimierz was annexed by Russia and served as a county seat for the province of Volhynia. After the Russian annexation, the social structure of the higher orders changed. Russian family dynasties founded on service to the tsars became the new owners of the estates, quarries, and timber houses. Jewish businessmen were able to lease and manage this land. Further down the class structure came the German merchants and the Jewish tradesmen, artisans, tailors, carpenters, butchers, and bakers living in the little ghetto of Wlodzimierz.

Zloczów is first mentioned in chronicles in the fifteenth century. In contrast to Wlodzimierz, which developed under Russian political and cultural influence, Zloczów entered the modern age under Austrian influence. A part of the Polish Commonwealth until the partitions of the late eighteenth century, Zloczów remained in the Habsburg Empire until it reverted back to Poland after World War I. It became part of the Soviet Ukraine after World War II and now lies within independent Ukraine.

Zloczów had a population of 30,000, roughly divided among Poles, Jews, and Ukrainians, between the two world wars. In September 1939, Hitler and Stalin attacked and divided Poland, with the Soviet Union annexing its eastern provinces, Western Ukraine. When Germany invaded the USSR almost two years later, in the summer of 1941, it occupied Zloczów—but not before the retreating Soviets massacred all the occupants of the local prison. Soon thereafter, Ukrainians went on an anti-Semitic rampage that lasted for three days. Three thousand Jews were murdered. At the same time, the Nazi authorities, together with the Ukrainian police, drove the Jews into the ghetto or systematically deported them to labor and death camps.

My father, a civil engineer, was put to work for the German army, the *Wehrmacht*, reconstructing war-damaged bridges and roads. He worked in that capacity until my mother arranged for his escape by hiding him in a hay wagon.

In September 1942, my family's situation changed again. The German army's defeat at Stalingrad was a turning point in the war. As the Soviets began their inexorable march toward Berlin, Poles and Ukrainians realized that the Germans were not invincible. Despite impending defeat, however, the Nazis rounded up Jews for extermination camps.

In the summer of 1943, my parents, two other family members, and I went into a bunker built under a barn in the village of Podhorce, near Zloczów. My younger brother and grandmother, and all other members of the family, had by then perished. I was seven when I entered the bunker; I was nine when I was liberated by the Soviet in June 1944.

1
OLGA

SHE WAS MY NANNY, and though I spent lots of time with her, it's hard for me to recall her face. I guess it's because I never remember her smiling. Her scowl made her face look like a cooked prune. But I did admire the precision of her grooming—especially the flawless way in which she coiled her long pigtails around her head.

Her protuberant eyes told me that she was on a terribly serious mission—to keep me as neat and perfect as possible by keeping her steady, critical eye on my activities, and reprimanding me whenever the opportunity arose. Good manners were, among other things, the foundation of perfection. So were keeping quiet when adults were talking, tucking a napkin under your chin when eating, chewing every little bit thoroughly, eating everything on your plate, never sticking out your tongue, or picking your nose. The sight of crumbs anywhere offended her. When I ate jam buns, the merest speck would be instantly wiped from my lips. I tried very hard to follow all her directions, but still she was not pleased. When I paused and chewed slowly, she sang a quiet incantation: a bite for me, a bite for you, a bite for your baby brother. But then she'd still complain, "Why are you eating so slowly? It's taking too long for you to eat. You have the manners of an aristocrat."

She was fastidious in all her work with me and never allowed other household help to enter her domain. She spent lots of time cleaning or tidying, washing or pressing my dresses and sorting big taffeta ribbons to match dress colors, scrubbing my room, mending my laundry or stockings, even tidying the porcelain doll's clothes.

One of the most serious activities was the weekly bath. Large galvanized pots of water sat on the coal-and-wood stove used for cooking and baking. One of those water pots was now heated for my bath. She poured the hot water into a galvanized tin tub and tested for the correct scrubbing temperature. I was plopped into the tub and mechanically handed two wooden spoons with which to paddle my kayak.

The warm water was marvelous. I sat happily for a long time as Olga soaped, scrubbed, and shampooed with bright yellow glycerin soap until my skin was steamy red and shiny. When I emerged, I was swallowed by a terrycloth bathing robe with a pompom monk's hood that hid my face. I felt light and virtuous, like an angel, while Olga recycled the water to a cauldron for laundry washing.

Olga had come to work for us from a nearby village when I was born and begun to take complete charge when the wet nurse left. She must have been about thirty, the age of my maiden aunt Sonia, but the two were never friends. Olga's single mission was my perfect appearance and behavior in our household and society, and she was invariably prepared for emergencies. When we went visiting, her survival kit included a bottle of lavender cologne, several embroidered handkerchiefs, and small pieces of worn linen sheets for potty emergencies, as privies only had rough squares of newspaper.

She was all business, no fun—my dress perfectly pressed, my curly hair just so with the big taffeta ribbon never out of place, my white shoes spotless, my posture perfect. Posture was crucial. One had to walk like a "proud Slav," which she demonstrated by walking with her shoulders thrown back, looking as if she had threaded a pole through her vertebrae. I was a hard assignment for her in a yard full of lumber, dirt, and mud.

Life was serious business. The big crucifix she wore symbolized her religious fervor. Her sacred mission was to save my body and soul, and I was doomed to follow her path to salvation.

I remember her taking away fun things and toys, and constantly scrubbing my dirty hands and fingernails. I also remember sitting on the little potty seat, listening to the trickling sound of urine and feeling its warm wetness on my vagina. I also loved the feel of the slow push of "number two" in the muscles of my rectum. Those were my secrets, over which Olga had no control. But the minute I finished and was ready to admire the fruits of my forbidden pleasures, the potty was quickly whisked away. Anything having to do with bodily functions was shameful, and I was forbidden to look. I was similarly forbidden to look at my "shameful parts" or have any dirty thoughts, but I discovered very early that I could think anything I wanted, and that Olga had no control over my fancy. I was also convinced that whatever was sternly forbidden must be very exciting, like all the other fun stuff I wasn't supposed to do. But if something was dirty or pleasurable, her prune face turned more disapproving. The source of pleasure disappeared, and it was back to business.

I was the neatest and most well behaved child in the family. I mirrored Olga's interpretation of my parents' wishes and was a true reflection of the stature of my noble grandfather, who as Olga always said had nothing Jewish in his looks or character. My grandfather, the family, our brick house (the only one in town), the lumber mills and warehouses, the fir forests where his workers felled trees—they almost made us Jewish royalty, and Olga was my minder, companion, and advisor. It was difficult for me to reflect that kind of perfection. I tried to please her and behave like a little adult, though she reprimanded me for one thing or other all the time.

My big reward for good behavior came on Sundays, a holy and mysterious time, when she took me to church. After breakfast, I changed into a Sunday dress and matching taffeta ribbon, the proper shoes and socks, and off we went. With Olga holding my hand, we began our pilgrimage to town— two penitent but very important people.

The small whitewashed Catholic church was near the center of town. We first cut through a cleared forest and then followed the main road, where droshkies rumbled in the dust and peasants strolled in their finery. In the spring, the main road was a kind of Ukrainian allée, with beautiful wild-flowering chestnut trees that created a fragrant white umbrella for the faithful. As we walked, men tipped their caps, and some peasant ladies bowed. Olga sometimes stopped to greet people she knew. Soon we were able to see the pointed spires of the church. We quickened our pace to get inside and sit down on the hard pews. The ceiling was a rounded dome, painted a wonderful heavenly azure, where pink angels and cherubs romped on delicate clouds. The ceiling was my favorite part of the church, and I imagined myself swinging from cloud to cloud with the cherubs, away from Olga and the solemn priests and choirboys below.

Our churchgoing routine changed with the seasons. Summers we left for vacation at my grandmother's in Zloczów. When we returned in the fall, the walk was more beautiful still. The sun shone lazily and warmly, and yellow leaves danced in the mild breezes. When rains came, we needed overcoats, umbrellas, and galoshes. I still managed to kick around as many chestnuts as I could, holding Olga's hand and not losing the rhythm of her pace.

Winter was a very special time. I believed her when she said that, then, the yardman glued stars unto the black sky, sprinkled diamonds into our garden, and painted windows with white, fernlike designs. Winter was also a time of miracles because of Christmas, the absolute high point of churchgoing for me.

As the holiday drew nearer, Olga grew more and more pious. If I had been especially good and obedient, I would be allowed to go to Christmas Mass and witness the miracle of miracles—Jesus born in a manger!

She spent many days in preparation for the event. I had a special winter-white dress with intricate tucks embroidered with little blue flowers, a white Persian lamb fur coat, white galoshes, a white knitted hat, mittens, and knitted stockings, all with matching embroidered white icicles that looked like ice flowers on window panes. I would also get to stay up late and not be punished, because I had prayed in church and was holy.

The pilgrimage was a serious event. Entering the church was especially wondrous. I gazed at the manger scene and imagined the clay figures and animals were real. I saw the calves and sheep moving around the manger as Joseph leaned over the cradle and Mary held the child's hand.

What fun it must be for the little baby to live in a warm

barn and romp around with sheep and calves, while angels with trumpets flew in the sky!

Then Olga told me a very frightening story. Seeing my wondrous, excited expression, she declared that the cherubic baby in the manger was really the Son of God, who long ago had suffered and died a terrible death by crucifixion. If I needed more proof of the horror, she would explain the story. She took me by the hand and led me to the altar to view the deed.

There, the statue of Jesus was very long and large, and his body ashen, dead white, almost violet in color. A crown of thorns was nailed to the top of his head. His face was in torment, his eyes shut. He looked so pained, so frightened, so sad.

But that was not the end of the horror. His hands and feet were nailed to the cross. Rivulets of scarlet blood were running down his palms and the soles of his feet. Blood also covered his body. I was especially terrified by the pain he must have endured in the palms of his hands and soles of his feet. Jarred by this figure, my mind could not make the connection between the tranquil manger scene, the soft warm hay, the loving figures of shepherds and animals, and the pain and terror of the statue.

Olga declared that the Jews had nailed him to the cross

because he was the Son of God! The devil was the father of the Jews. He made them do it, and the Jews would be punished for the Lord's terrible death. She reported very matter-of-factly how, after making him carry that heavy cross all around town, the Jews had barbarously crucified him—with his mother watching, no less.

Somehow, in the course of the story, it became clear to me that it was my fault that Jesus had suffered and been murdered. But how could I be responsible for his fate? A knot of pity and fear formed in my stomach, and a shiver went down my spine. I was frightened and could no longer enjoy the heavenly chanting of the little boys' choir or the procession of the priests. Even the smoke coming out of the incense boxes spoke of danger and warned of bad things to come.

The priest droned on in a mysterious language that seemed to accuse me. I was cold. My knees felt clammy and stiff as I knelt on the clay floor and prayed to go home.

Finally, Mass was over, and the church doors opened to freedom. The night was bright with stars. The narrow paths trodden into deep snow were icy and treacherous. Our path was framed by snow-covered branches in which a thousand sparks were gleaming. Only the sparkling stars and the jingling of sleigh bells down the road pushed me forward. Olga was taking me to our peaceful house, away from the scene of that bloody murder. Again, she was my savior. I held her hand tightly and skipped home, listening instead to the sounds of my white rubber galoshes squeaking on paths of glistening, crunchy snow.

2
PARADISE LOST

OUR HOUSE was on the outskirts of Wlodzimierz, near rolling meadows and pine forests. Behind the orchard, filled with apple, cherry, and plum trees, fields of buckwheat mixed with the sharp smell of fresh hay and meadow grass. When a breeze drifted across the meadows it filled our yard and garden with perfume. The aroma filled me with comfort and happiness, and sometimes made me giddy. Peasant fields, visible in the distance, seemed like embroidered napkin patches painted with blooming poppies, cornflowers, and buttercups.

It was a time of safety, delight, and excitement—but too little adventure. I could hear the sounds of summer outside the kitchen window. If only I could leave the garden and the yard, and run in the meadows and fields! Better still would be to run, to the secret place beyond, a scary cemetery where dead people lived.

It was close to the meadows and up a little hill—a forbidden, mysterious place. When I was especially good and promised my teenage cousin Pipa to keep a secret, he would take me to play there with his street friends. Pipa, strong and ruddy with smiling eyes, was my hero. As Olga often remarked, he was very mischievous, but since, as with my grandfather, his features were not all Jewish, she approved of him.

I felt very special and proud when he chose me rather than his sister Bella to share in his adventures with the street boys. Pipa began introducing me to his friends slowly. When cherry trees were laden with fruit and picking season came, the boys came to our orchards to help with the cherry harvest. They would be rewarded with a basket of cherries for their work, and a cherrystone-eating contest began. After eating the cherries, each boy made a separate pile of his pits, and the contest ended with Pipa counting the piles and rewarding the winner with candy or chocolate. I also got some cherries but never ate fast enough to win. But that didn't matter. I was thrilled to be a working member of the group.

I particularly remember one time (I must have been about five) when Pipa asked me to play with the local boys beyond the family compound. To become a member of the group, I had to look less "girlie" and roll down my knee socks, take off the taffeta hair ribbon, and stick it in a pocket.

It was a time of mystery and adventure for a little girl in fancy clothes. The boys accepted me and encouraged me to run wildly with them and be initiated to the secrets of their cemetery games. Once we got there, Władek became our leader in a serious game of hide and seek. Taller and ganglier than Pipa, he was a skinny, disheveled kid, one of the children of our local lumberman. Władek had no shoes and ran barefoot. At least his toes could feel the pleasures of country life —the hot sand of the dirt roads, the spongy grass of the pastures, and the rock-strewn earth. Władek was a child of nature who drank in the sounds and smells of the fluid Ukrainian plain. For me he was becoming another hero.

As we chased around the graves and tombstones, as the smallest I tried hard to keep up with the gang. Władek took me under his wing and occasionally grabbed my hand to help me when the going got tough. He said that the dead people inside the graves would chase and catch us if I didn't run quickly and hide. I was afraid but at the same time felt very grown up and pleased that I had been accepted as a comrade in arms.

The cemetery was a big, unkempt place with little rounded houses, some with columns, some with upright graves of granite or marble, decorated with wreaths and flowers and serious, official photographs of the dead reflecting the wealth and importance of the local families. The designs and forms of the wooden crosses were wonderfully intricate, with sculpted flowers and airy birds. I was relieved that the place was flowery and friendly and there were no heavy chunks of wood with the murdered Jesus. The important plots were surrounded by cast-iron fences with locks and chains, while the plots of the poor had low enclosures of carved wood.

I remember having long, serious conversations with Władek about the dead people. One time, he said that he had seen a naked man run out of his grave in the morning, a very unusual occurrence as the dead came out only at night and only in fine weather. On very cold, frosty nights, the dead remained in their graves. But in warm weather, especially when the sky was bright with stars and moonshine, the dead would come out of their little houses and talk about their still living friends and relatives. The dead also kept their eye on the behavior of their kin and friends, and advised Saint Peter who should end up in heaven with the angels and who should be punished by the devil in hell. Władek explained that this was a Christian cemetery, which was different from the Jewish one on the other side of town, because all dead Jewish people were children of the devil and automatically went to hell. The story Olga had told me many times was thus confirmed by Władek. I was Jewish. How could I end up with the angels and be saved from the fires of hell? I thought about that problem all the time.

One day, while resting after a long run, Władek took my hand and began to speak in secret and intimate whispers.

"I will show you something you have never seen before! A giant thing that only boys have. It is red and long and fat and its in my pants. When I take it out, and pee, it will spray like a fountain!"

I blinked and swallowed, and waited.

"I will show my cock to you only if you roll down your panties and pee beside me."

The fires of hell were surely coming now, I thought and felt my cheeks burning. But I was intrigued by his description of this hidden instrument. It seemed wild and scary, and I wanted to see. I quickly rolled up my dress, pulled down my panties, and showed him my little vagina, which would not pee. He pulled out his penis. What Wladek said was true. It was long and thick and, as he waved it from side to side, it peed like crazy!

The other boys pointed to my little vagina and laughed, while admiring Wladek's great weapon. I began to feel helpless and ashamed, and wished Olga were there to reprimand the boys and rescue me. I commanded myself not to cry, but my face grew red and sweaty. I pulled up my panties and knee socks, and ran home as quickly as my feet would carry me. My dress was rumpled and smudged, my face dirty, my knees bruised, my arms scratched.

Worst of all, I'd somehow lost face with the boys and felt they were no longer my friends.

The cemetery adventure was a deep secret I could not share with anyone. Would Pipa, my hero, keep it? I never ventured out to the cemetery again.

3
GRANDFATHER JACOB

I REMEMBER my grandfather Jacob as a very tall, erect, and handsome man. His soft blue eyes smiled and sparkled, and his shiny silver hair, beard, and handlebar mustache filled me with anticipation. Elegantly dressed in three-piece English tweeds, he wore a Timber Merchant's Guild button on his lapel that spoke of his social standing and authority. After lunch, when I was cozy on his lap, he asked me to tell him about my games and activities. I was intoxicated by the spicy aroma of cologne that rose from his jacket and the smell of his shiny leather boots. I was the youngest and prettiest of the grandchildren, and although I wasn't certain that I was his favorite, I was sure he liked me a lot and was my friend. I could tell that from his smile and the warmth and comfort of his lap. His long fingers alternated between playfully stroking the curls in my hair and tickling my ribs.

Grandfather Jacob came from a family of rabbis and merchants—a union of ancient piety and savvy capitalism. He'd begun his lumber business at the turn of the century by managing the accounts of Russian nobility who'd lost interest in overseeing their forests and hunting grounds in Volhynia. Alcohol and gambling debts eventually forced the sale of their estates to him and other Jews. Seeing a window of opportunity, Jewish accountants and business people were able to buy up logging rights and become timber merchants.

By the 1890s, our family owned outright or managed thousands of acres of forestland in Volhynia stretching deep into the Jewish Pale. Because of their prominence in the lumber business, they were part of a tiny Jewish elite that was given honorary citizenship in the Russian Empire and exempted from certain laws that applied to the lesser Jewish community. Grandpa Jacob told us that our family had settled in the area in the late Middle Ages, after being driven east by the Church. The family settled in Wlodzimierz, a county seat of the Eastern Church.

By the start of the twentieth century, the family's

sawmills and forests employed hundreds of Jewish and Ukrainian timber cutters. The workforce was international—Polish, Russian, or German, depending on the project. Workers felled pines, assembled them into rafts, and poled them down the Dnieper toward Kiev, where sawmills turned them into lumber for Russian industry. Grandfather was officially contracted by the Russian throne to build steps for the public buildings in St. Petersburg, as well as to supply ties for railroad construction. His business flourished, and he was awarded the medal of Timber Merchant of the First Guild of the province of Volhynia and granted citizenship in the Russian Empire, a rare honor for a Jew.

Our house straddled the line between town and country. It had been built in the early 1900s on the outskirts of town, close to the lumber mill, carpenter shop, and warehouses. It was the first brick house in Wlodzimierz, and a curiosity for the locals who would drive out in their droshkies on Sunday to view the latest construction wonder. It was very large and commodious enough to have one apartment for each family—us, my grandparents, and my uncle's family. The windows were larger than usual, and the roof attracted special attention, as it was made from gleaming German copper.

Citizenship, social and financial standing, and brains

allowed Jacob's sons to enter Kiev University, a great accomplishment for Jews after World War I. In short, along with the two Jewish doctors and several government officials, Grandfather Jacob was considered Jewish royalty in Wlodzimierz Wolynski.

The governor of the province sent a messenger every afternoon to inquire about his well-being. The following morning, Grandfather dispatched a beadle to return the governor's gesture and bestow gifts on him and his family. Jacob's world was safe and beautiful, his life calm and well regulated. The family lived in quiet contentment and predictability in that backwater Ukrainian town.

The old merchant rose early, toured some mills, oversaw government business, lunched, drank tea, changed into a velvet raspberry robe with tassels, and napped. He spent his evenings at the local restaurant or tavern, discussing business with cronies and government officials over good food and plenty of drink, and distributing favors to smooth the challenges of future projects. Soon, Jacob became wealthy enough to take holidays at Baltic resorts and mineral cures and waters at German and Czech spas. There were also business and public relations trips. Each spring after Passover, accompanied by a rabbi, two accountants, and both sons, he traveled far and wide to teach the boys the business and introduce them to timber merchants in Lithuania and Germany. The family visited merchant homes for dinner and prayed with them in synagogue, where a shabbes goy (a gentile for the Sabbath) stood at the ready to open, shut, and carry umbrellas in inclement weather, a service unheard of in the hinterlands of Ukraine.

Women in our family were modest and charitable. They acquired only two new outfits a year—one for Passover, and one for Rosh Hashana—and never wore makeup or jewelry unless going on holiday. All of us, especially the children, were highly scrutinized by Jews and Gentiles alike. Our mandate was perfect appearance and perfect behavior on all public outings, and since Olga was in charge, there was no hope of freedom.

One brilliant and peaceful early September day, we were ready to celebrate a big event—Grandpa Jacob's seventieth birthday. Grandmother, as always, sat on her throne, an upholstered rocking chair at the far end of the kitchen, and, like a captain on a bridge, shouted orders to the cook and the maid and anyone else who came into the kitchen for the preparation of the feast. Tables had been laid out in the backyard, the women and servants busy carrying food from the kitchen, the children given the job of chasing away flies. Soon the guest of honor arrived with his assistant, Asher, who was dressed in a formal dark suit—his little pot-belly covered with a flowered waistcoat—gleaming boots, and a shiny top hat. He resembled a court jester, and performed mischievous tricks for the children. Asher's hearty laughter, a few coins he found in my hair, and the yelps and shouts of family and friends got the party going.

Somehow, Grandfather Jacob didn't look well that day. His eyes were not twinkling, his hair was a bit disheveled, and his mustache was dull. Most striking to me was his change in posture. My knight in shining armor, usually erect as a rod, suddenly appeared bent over, stooped, half his size. Olga remarked that, on that day, Grandfather looked Jewish. When I asked why he wasn't standing straight, he smiled and reassured me with a gentle pat that it was only gout.

The next day, that energetic man took to bed. His illness lasted a long time and was shrouded in mystery, with lots of commotion, hushed voices, the pungent smell of medicine and alcohol, doctors coming and going, all attending the patient. Two specialists in gold-rimmed spectacles came from Lwów to consult with the local doctor, and various treatments were prescribed without success. When the latest medicines didn't work, folk medicine was tried.

The local *feltscher* (male nurse) stroked Jacob's pale body hourly with rubbing alcohol compresses, while my father held his face within centimeters of a boiling pot of potatoes to ease his breathing. Another popular cure was "cupping". I was allowed to watch this magic show. The feltscher brought in a black lacquered suitcase filled with little cups. He set up a table, covered with a clean sheet, and placed his instruments on top. With the flair of a magician, he lit a long match and put one hand behind his back while, with the other, he ignited each cup, sucking the air out to create a vacuum. The little cups hissed, crackled, and popped as he swished them dramatically and placed them in rows on Grandfather's bare back. The little glass cups attached themselves, sucking the poor man's blood to the surface, turning the skin bright red. This ancient procedure was believed to help with circulation by sucking the phlegm and the disease to the surface, where it could evaporate.

My grandfather's back, with the cups laid in even rows, looked to me like a muffin pan. Alas, that didn't work. Prayer became the only source of salvation. The rabbi came twice each day to sit with the men and pray.

Grandmother's permanently panicked face and lifeless

eyes peeked out from the vestibule in terror. She stopped men coming out of his room to ask questions, which they ignored. She continued to wring her hands and sigh and take sedative valerian drops. Her daughter, Sonia, allowed herself occasional tears, even though emotions had to be kept in check and crying was not permitted. Olga was in charge of me and made sure I followed her script. I was to keep silent and polite, and my expression was to be appropriately serious.

Autumn was my favorite time of the year. The days were molten gold and silver and very brief. The yellow sun was still hot but already very slanted. It turned red and set very quickly after a short day.

Swarms of ravens circled the sky as the sun rose from a bed of silver and mist. I spent most of the time in the garden on a bright yellow bench. The garden was a good place to be when I felt like getting out of the way and being alone with my thoughts amid the birdsong and the whispering of the breeze in the branches.

The yellow bench was also a good place to look at picture books and play with toys. I imitated medical procedures that were going on in Grandfather's bedroom by cutting worms in half with scissors. One day, our cat mauled a sparrow in the undergrowth of the bushes. The bird's head was scalped, and its naked skull resembled a gooseberry. Olga said the bird was martyred, and I dressed it for its funeral with a cap of lace scraps and a white shroud. I put the bird in a chocolate box and buried it near the meadows while a red-and-green rooster cocked its head and observed my activities.

Autumn leaves already covered the ground, and the fields were yellow and prickly. Although the earth hurt my feet when I ran in sandals, I loved the acrid smell of the fields. The boys were roasting potatoes and shouting for me to join them. The smell of roasted potato skins on fire, blending with the strong smell of mowed hay and grass, drew me, but Olga's nasty face peering from the porch stopped me. Still skipping at the garden's edge, I angrily kicked small pieces of lumber and patches of dry earth.

I tried to understand what was happening inside. Olga said Grandfather was very ill and dying, and no medicine could cure him. But only birds died. I knew that life was eternal. But Olga knew better. Since we all lived in a perpetual state of sin on earth, perhaps Grandfather, like Jesus, would be redeemed in heaven. I knew all about the death of Jesus. As I remembered, no one had tried to help Jesus or save him. Jesus had been young and strong and carried his cross, before he had been nailed to it. But Grandfather was not suffering and didn't need resurrection. He was resting in his comfortable bed, there was no blood, and lots of doctors and rabbis were trying to help him! I was befuddled and did not believe her.

On good days, I was allowed to see him. Olga would permit me to wear her coral beads, to ward off the Evil Eye. His eyes lit up to greet me, and he would weakly extend his warm, liver-spotted hand, so I could squeeze it and play with his long fingers. Patches of autumn sunlight peeked through the curtain as it moved in the breeze, producing a magic show of light and sound on the Kazakh carpet. I felt happy and safe sitting next to his bed in complete silence, and wanted to stay there forever.

He did not improve. He seemed longer and much thinner, he wheezed and coughed, and his skin soon changed to the color of lilac. Olga had been right again! The doctors announced that the end was near. His illness and ultimate death were shrouded in the same mystery and solemnity as those of Jesus, but were less frightening because he was my grandfather and I loved him. Also, this time I was convinced that his death was not my fault or that of other Jews.

One day, after prayers, the rabbi declared that children

could not share the same roof with the dead, so Olga and I were sent packing to a neighbor's house. Grandfather died during the night. The rabbi said that the burial could not be delayed and had to take place immediately, as leaving a body unburied was a humiliation for the dead.

Part of Grandfather Jacob's timber empire contained a carpentry shop that produced coffins, cradles, and kitchen tables. Wining and dining state officials for government contracts, and travel for the timber business, gave him enough headaches, so he and his brother-in-law, Rabbi Ezra, who had a hard time making ends meet in the synagogue, had thought of a sure bread-and-butter business close to home.

"Children are born, people have to eat, and they have to die," Rabbi Ezra had opined. "You know, before I went to yeshiva, I worked in a carpenter's shop in Rovno."

"I have plenty of timber, plenty of labor, and plenty of space!" Jacob had replied enthusiastically. "You, Ezra, will run the shop! This business is a perfect hedge for uncertainties. Don't forget, I was a soldier when the Russian and German empires mobilized and began the slow end of our great Austro-Hungary. Something can happen again. Pilsudski is dead. I hear the Germans are stripping Jews of citizenship. It's always good to have a commodity hedge business in this world."

The carpentry shop had been a steady moneymaker from day one. Orders, from both Jews and Gentiles, had come in from neighboring towns, and the shop soon employed five carpenters and three apprentices. Uncle Ezra's cheeks were shiny and red, and he always smelled of fresh wood shavings.

When Jacob's end was imminent, Uncle Ezra had ordered Nikita, the master carpenter, to begin work on a coffin. The shop was a busy place, conveniently located behind the orchard and our house on the way to the Gentile cemetery where I had lost my innocence with Wladek. Uncle Ezra shuttled between prayers for his brother-in-law and the carpentry shop to assure the family that Jacob's coffin would be suitable enough to respect the family and Jacob's brilliant and honest reputation in the timber business. Nikita chiseled and carved a magnificent coffin of oaken boards with silver shields of David, and attached black-and-gold tassels to the corners. A student from the Talmud Torah carved a verse from an ancient prayer for the dead, and chanted for three days. I saw the coffin in the yard the day Olga and I were exiled from the house, and for the first time I was terribly frightened. It looked too spacious for Grandfather alone, and I was sure that someone else would be put in to keep him company.

"They will take him away! I will never see him again!" I cried to Olga.

I knew that he would live in the Jewish cemetery, and I wasn't sure that the people buried there had as much fun at night as in Wladek's playground, but Olga assured me that he would join the righteous Christians in heaven.

"Life is a dung heap, the world a brothel, and people a lot of crooks," sang Nikita with a cackling laugh as he polished the intricate corners of the coffin.

"We are all dead men, we are in the hands of pharaoh," replied Ezra.

"Everything is transitory. We're here today and gone tomorrow. Some things, like pearls, medals, and coffins, only age, but people, dogs, and animals die," Nikita remarked philosophically. "Wipe your tears, and thank God for giving us a chance to taste this and that at the feast of life."

"Eat something, Nikita, and let's drink to Jacob's full life and the coming of the Messiah," Ezra interrupted. "If a person is dead, that's for a long time. If he's stupid, that's forever." Nikira sneered.

It was a sleepless night for Olga and me in our neighbor's house. When the roosters crowed, our eyes were already wide open. I cried and cried and stomped my feet. I was not mourning for Grandfather but was determined to watch the funeral procession. Since Olga also wanted to say good-bye to Grandfather, she agreed that we would follow, slowly and stealthily, to watch the march of the bereaved.

Our house was far from the Jewish cemetery, and since it was too difficult for the pallbearers to carry the coffin on their shoulders, a hearse and a driver were hired. Motyl, the baker's assistant, got the job. My father and uncle led the procession, with the women following behind like sheep, supporting one another in their grief. Motyl, dressed elegantly in black with cravat and top hat, was ready for action and the hearse followed. I remember the mourners clearly, the men in black coats and hats, the women in their fox collars, some with shawls over their heads. I also remember two beggars walking beside the group, rattling their tins, pleading for money.

The procession slowly passed the park where I played with my friends. The ground was covered with golden leaves, the birches swayed in the breeze, the linden trees shimmered. The procession passed the synagogue, where the group stopped to pray, and then continued up the hill to the cemetery. The remaining relatives and mourners followed behind.

The pallbearers entered the cemetery gates and carried the coffin along a narrow path, with tombstones on both sides, inscribed in Yiddish, Hebrew, and Polish. The people, the trees, and the cemetery beggars stood silent.

As the rabbi and the chanters continued their prayers for Grandfather, the women wept, brokenhearted. "The Lord hath given, and the Lord taketh away. Blessed is the name of the Lord," the rabbi chanted. "Grant perfect rest beneath the sheltering wings of Your presence among the holy and the pure."

Olga was confused by the rabbi's explanation and gave me her own interpretation. "Grandfather doesn't have to wait for the Messiah. Lord Jesus is the Messiah and has already been resurrected. Jacob's soul is going directly to St. Peter and the angels, and we just have to pray that he is happy at last, and that we see him again when we get there."

Bewildered and upset, I began pulling on Olga's coat to take me home, but instead we continued to follow the procession. I was distressed that the march was so different from others in the town square. I was also sad and couldn't quite understand why. The coffin was lowered into the grave. My father, uncle, and other relatives took turns shoveling earth on the coffin, which echoed with an unforgettable sound.

Uncle Ezra said that Grandfather would rest in peace until the coming of the Messiah, but Olga said the Messiah was already here. If Grandfather was going straight to heaven, how could he make his way out of the coffin and all that earth? Why were all the women shaking and weeping? Terrified, I hid behind Olga's skirts, afraid that Motyl would charge at us with the horses to punish us for following the funeral march.

At last Olga took me home. First she had me drink hot cocoa with no skin on the milk, then a *kogelmogel*—a creamy thick, sweet mixture of egg yolk, sugar, and butter—and finally she put me into bed, correctly stretching out my arms on top of the covers. After she left the room, I permitted myself to cry and shake with fear, eventually drifting into a child's deep sleep.

4
LWÓW OPERA

ONE RAILWAY LINE connected the
towns of Zloczów and Wlodzimierz with the great cosmo-
politan town of Lwów, designated by the Habsburgs as the
capital of the Galician region. Lwów is where my parents
courted, and I am overcome by a sense of relief and pleasure
when I permit myself to understand that they had a blessed
and normal life before the war. I am able to see that old
multinational city as a great and lively place not entirely colored by my own sense of loss and suffering. Lwów was a
Polish and Jewish island in a sea of Ukrainian peasants; it was
a colorful provincial capital, with blurred borders that possessed dignity and charm. Never mind that Emperor Franz

Joseph was dead, that Józef Piłsudski ruled Poland. Mother and Father always believed that they were proud citizens of the Habsburg Empire.

Lwów was a bastion of culture and politics, and a window into civilized Europe. Beside the red and white flags of the Polish Republic and, rarely, the occasional blue and yellow of nationalist Ukrainians, the yellow and black of the Habsburg monarchy still fluttered in public places. Portraits of Emperor Franz Joseph stared benignly at customers in cafes and elegant restaurants. Surely, a combination of these colors could do no harm to the new Polish state. The many languages and nationalities, the appreciation of local differences, made Lwów the Little Vienna of the East, a partner in Europe's civilizing mission. Nostalgia for empire reigned.

The Europa coffeehouse was close to the train station, where Father and Mother would meet when they reached Lwów from different directions. The minute they entered the Europa, they stopped being emancipated Polish Jews and became Jewish Poles, looking for roast pork on the menu. The coffeehouse had a vaulted, smoky ceiling and mysterious dark niches where chess players sat hunkered down to their games. The bar, full of multicolored bottles and sparkling glasses, was presided over by two bosomy blond barmaids.

Nearby, the old waiter, Otto, a little shaky at the knee, his toes turned up, a napkin over his forearm, shuffled among the customers. Otto had worked in the Europa since the days of the Habsburgs. He'd wanted to be a draftsman at the Lwów Polytechnic, but had run out of money and been lucky to find work at the Europa.

He didn't like his work. He was much happier reading the newspapers, gossiping, and discussing politics with customers. Otto knew my father and mother and their families, remembered the dates of their arrival in Lwów, and saved a special table for them not too close to the gypsy violins. Although the town had changed, he told the same stories about Lwów's more glorious days, comparing the fall of the Habsburgs to the fall of the Romans.

"I remember when our city was a kaleidoscope of music and color," he sighed. "Soldiers in bright uniforms promenaded in the park. I remember the blue and red trousers of the cavalrymen, the coffee-colored jackets of the artillery, the black saloon pants of the militia, the policemen in feathered hats or helmets with gold pompoms and glittering golden Habsburg eagles.

"There was money for public service, the gardeners were paid on time, the parks were well tended and full of flowers, our visitors strolled arm in arm, and the birds chirped Austrian tunes.

"The town still hangs in a fog of nostalgia for the good old days, and some peasants actually believe that the old emperor moved from Vienna to Warsaw, and has only changed the colors of uniforms and emancipated his Poles. But one cannot fill one's stomach on the past," Otto sighed.

In Lwów, my parents allowed themselves to be charming and exotic, and felt themselves beyond nationality. They imagined that they spoke many languages, knew their way around most watering spas, and had friends and relatives all over the world. They promenaded the boulevards of Lwów, dressed in the latest fashion. Old photographs suggest they were a beautiful pair. She—solidly built, broad-shouldered, elegant and attractive, tailored with severity and restraint— wears a felt hat. A feather waves above it like an arrogant peacock's tail, cutting a fine slanting line across her brow. The brim comes down on the right side of her neat hair and sweeps upward on the left like the stern of a boat. Her gloved fingers hover slightly above the sleeve of my father's overcoat, barely touching him. He is also nattily dressed, stiff, well turned out, more than a head taller, and with a homburg on his head. His face is serious, resolute, almost lugubrious. His eyes are elongated and dreamy.

Jankel Geller, now Jacques Gallier, a very extraordinary uncle on my father's side who had settled in Lwów, was their very special friend.

He was an agent for a textile firm in Lódz, the Polish Manchester, and had an impressive business card with a gold border and a geometric emblem shaped like a heap of diamonds. The card read: *Jacques Gallier, Authorized Representative, General Agent and Accredited Wholesaler, Lwów and the Province of Galicia.*

He would hold out his card with an apologetic, childlike laugh: "*Nu*, what? A man has to live somehow."

His real claim to fame was that he was also an actor in the Yiddish theatre, for which he traveled extensively to Prague, Vienna, Berlin, and Paris. His manners were courtly. He dressed like a dandy: a jacket with padded shoulders and a high, old-fashioned collar, patent-leather shoes, and a derby. He had the assurance of a count and a way with women, invariably said something nice to the most unattractive ones, and was rumored to have had many affairs with famous actresses. Already quite old in the 1930s, he worked stubbornly at straightening his stoop when greeting my parents in Lwów.

In the tradition of the old-time Jewish theater, he would lapse into Germanized Yiddish, particularly if he spoke of culture or history. Bloated with cultural superiority and an air of European celebrity, he usually met my parents at the Jewish Culture Club on Walowa Street on the evening of their arrival in town. He greeted them warmly and then proceeded to survey the club disdainfully, grimacing at the smells of herring, garlic, and cheap tobacco, and criticizing the shrill voices of *schlemiels* who endlessly discussed literature. He always treated waiters with a special kind of magnanimous condescension. "Excuse me. The tea is cold. I ask you to bring me, right away, hot tea: hot tea, that means the essence also must be very, very hot. Not just the water. Thank you very much." My parents liked him because he was something of a celebrity, a facilitator of their trysts, and their entrée into Lwów's high culture.

The Lwów Opera was truly a palace of culture. Designed by a Polish architect, with an auditorium that seated 1,100 people, the house had opened in 1900 and rivaled that of any important European city. Typically ornate and eclectic in late nineteenth-century style, it boasted Corinthian columns and classical statues of Comedy and Tragedy, as well as bronze muses in rococo settings.

My father, who belonged to the Patriotic Circle of Poles of the Mosaic Faith, was in love with Richard Wagner's music. Lohengrin was the big hit, and seats for the parterre were difficult to get. Not only did Uncle Jacques provide them, he also provided discreet accommodations in his apartments, with reliable alibis for sleeping arrangements. My parents were in love with each other and with life. Lwów represented the familiar in the midst of variability, a constant in the midst of change, the dependable in the midst of the unaccustomed.

Music was everywhere. Restaurants were classy and swell, their tables covered with starched tablecloths and upright napkins. They were filled with impeccably and elegantly dressed people copying the styles of the fashionistas of the day, the Duke and Duchess of Windsor. Women wore elegant suits with small, fresh bunches of purple violets pinned to their lapels, stylish feathered cloche hats, handmade pointed shoes, and shimmering silk stockings. Men were just as fashion-conscious, decked out in the softest and finest British woolens, bowler hats, and walking sticks with ivory or gold handles.

Their clothes were tailored by Motek, whose fame was unparalleled. There was no one like him in the world. He managed a fashion house on Kruszelnicka Avenue, the Madison Avenue of Lwów, a broad, tree-lined thoroughfare, with public monuments and ornamental plantings framed by elegant historic buildings. The avenue was built in the late nineteenth and early twentieth centuries by Polish, Ukrainian, and Jewish architects and contractors. A crown jewel of a street, it remained the central promenade of the city's burghers, whatever their nationality.

It was rumored that Motek knew the measurements of all his customers by heart because he could not read and write and had trouble writing figures. The tape measure also gave him trouble, so he used a piece of string and tied knots for sizes. When he picked up his scissors, it was as though his customers were standing in front of him, and he had no trouble cutting out their coats, trousers, and waistcoats.

Little samples of every piece of cloth he had ever sewn were pinned to one wall as badges of his tailoring excellence. He knew what kind of suit he made for each client and was proud of his craftsmanship. He lived in a world of his own. When he wasn't working, he was busy trying to picture the dimensions of his customers, to remember all their bellies, chests, and thighs. Although the fashion shop on Kruszelnicka employed seamstresses, dressmakers, and tailors, Motek was the style setter of Lwów. From time to time, he did make a little mistake and was left with enough material to make a suit for himself. He had no problem with that. It was only right for a tailor of his reputation.

Warm memories fill me when I remember the sweet tales of my parents' courtship. Lwów must have been curious and exciting, a strange mix of eccentrics, con artists, frauds, and hoaxes, a place where preening was more important than substance. Through their stories, they not only pined for it—the city of their youth—but for their young selves.

5
FURS AND SILVER

OUR BIG HOUSE stood proudly amid the calm and silence of our small street on the outskirts of town. Its chimneys touched the sky higher than our neighbor's on the corner. It stood golden in the sun and pale green in the shade. If I had been allowed to walk down the street alone, I would eventually have reached open country, where meadows dotted with tall stacks of hay heralded the autumn harvest. Further on were fields, followed by brush and tempting dark hills and woods stretching to the horizon.

The day was autumnally mild. I wandered free in the garden or sat on the egg-yellow bench, swinging my bare feet in the dust, pleased with the shimmer of linden trees and the flutter of poplars. As day was dying, I could see lights in the house and smell the warmth of a tranquil evening at home. That meant eating a supper of soup and sandwiches with the family, discussing the day's activities, reading fairytales, always with a moral to frighten me into good behavior, and being tucked into bed by Olga, whom mother supervised with glances from the door.

But that evening, news from father's magic box, the Telefunken radio, disrupted the normal routine. The radio's gothic shape and richly warm mahogany always brought excitement and escape to a different and important world. A warm wind was wandering through the room when I came home that afternoon. The magic box was whistling, squeaking, and shouting in a strange language about Hitler and the Sudetenland. Pretty soon the whole family gathered around, listening, as the radio wheezed and crackled and occasionally faded altogether. My uncle managed to silence the beeps and whistling sounds with a good slap to the box while Father nervously puffed on his cigarettes and explained to us that the Germans and Hitler would be marching on Poland, and that there would be war. Grown-ups discussed strange-sounding words like *Anschluss, Atlee, Chamberlain, Stalin,* and *Churchill.*

Soon, war was declared, the Germans invaded Poland, and our life changed forever. I became afraid of the strange whistling sounds of languages I did not know. Shopping trips to Lwów were postponed, and we no longer went for long walks or constant rounds of visits. Shopping in the village market, meal preparation, and mid-day dinners were no longer discussed in keen detail. I was sure that it was all the fault of that magic Telefunken box, which had suddenly become more important for the grown-ups than my routine. On the other hand, because the adults were distracted, I didn't have to obey all of Olga's reprimands and orders.

Every day, father read many newspapers and searched for news about our destiny. He told us about a state dinner in the Kremlin where Ribbentrop and Molotov agreed to make peace, but Germany and Russia attacked Poland anyway and occupied large parts of southern and western territory. News bulletins were posted all over town. There was panic, and people started to run away, terrified by the short-wave radio's ominous and threatening war chatter and Hitler's speeches about "the complete annihilation of the Jews." Father kept repeating the words "annihilation of the Jews," and the family was especially distressed by the news. I kept asking what the words meant and all he could say was that we were Jewish, and that that was very bad now. How could we be Jewish, if we were Polish? I sensed that we were somehow different from our neighbors. Our house was bigger, and we dressed in nicer clothes, we were quieter, and I had a nanny. But I was Polish, we all spoke Polish, I recited Polish nursery rhymes, and my parents even allowed me to go to church with Olga. But I was Jewish also, and perhaps Olga was right, and I did murder Jesus? Father was panic-stricken, overwhelmed by dread, his hands trembling as he continually puffed on cigarettes.

My uncle Schloyme did not want to abandon our house. "We are trapped here," he said. "We can't run away. It's impossible to get to the sea from here. Besides, what should we do with our house and possessions?"

Nobody in our family paid much attention to father, and his brother Schloyme blamed his panic on weak nerves. "I remember the Germans from the First War," he said calmly. "They behaved like military gentlemen and were proud of keeping perfect order. Their military bands gave concerts in the park. Some people in Lwów are saying there will be no war, that they will just let us off with a scare, while others are saying that Lwów will be defended by the Poles and the army will mount effective resistance."

"A big battle will be fought there," answered father. "Trenches are being dug, and even old Jews with *peyes* are helping dig. We are doomed."

Soon the skies were black with planes. When the alarm sounded, everyone thought it was just a test, and hundreds died before they could reach shelters. Bombs landed on roads, trains, and buildings. We heard terrible crashing sounds, and saw roofs on fire. Roads were littered with broken-down cars and dead horses. Planes dove down and shot at people. Fleeing crowds took cover in ditches and ran on, ignoring the groans of the wounded.

I tried to understand the panic and course of events but couldn't. Why the bombs, the fire, and the smoke? Perhaps it's just a big circus coming to town with noise and fire? Are soldiers coming to our house, our garden? Why would soldiers be coming to Wlodzimierz? What would they want with the piles of timber, apple and cherry orchards, and meadows where I watched cows and horses wander and graze, and gathered cornflowers and poppies?

After much time and many quiet and intense conversations, important decisions were made. Mother decided that our little family and Olga would move to Zloczów to be with her parents—but only for a very short time, until things got better.

She wanted to go home to her mother and father. Trains were still running, and it was decided that our family, and of course Olga, would travel to Grandpa Mendel and Babcia Hancia's house. I loved the idea of living in their large and beautiful apartment in a modern yellow house. The ceiling of the front hall was painted blue, white, and pink, with clouds and cherubs romping among flowered garlands. I especially liked the cast-iron staircase and intricate ironwork balconies overlooking a small, densely treed town park. I jumped up and down at the thought of Grandpa Mendel and his hearty laugh, coming home each evening with pockets full of colored marzipans and chocolates in the shapes of animals and flowers! Mother was happier and said with certitude, "Now that England has declared war on Germany, all these troubles will end very soon, and we will be back in our house in no time."

Father said that Uncle Schloyme would continue to run the lumber business, and the family, including his unmarried sister Sonia and Grandmother, would remain in the house. Since the house and the family were in danger and had to be secured against peasants and soldiers roaming about the town, the gardener Tomasz and his wife Marfa would live in our apartment for extra protection. If things got really dangerous, Tomasz would build a shelter in the root cellar, which contained barrels of pickles and sauerkraut, bins of potatoes and beets, and huge, empty leather trunks. There, Tomasz and Marfa would care for and protect the remaining family. I was fascinated with Tomasz's strange looks, the flame-red beard that covered his face in a funny way because it didn't grow out in straight hairs, like ordinary beards, but in tufts of red wool. He also had a big hat made of cat fur, which he wore all year round. It smelled of sweat, dead animals, raw leather, and tallow. Though I was worried that the smell would live in our house forever, I really liked Tomasz, his beard, and his hat.

Of course, Markus would also live in the house. I liked the idea of my two favorite people, Tomasz and Markus, actually living in our house. Markus was a superior servant with a great aptitude for domestic tasks, which he performed with enormous satisfaction. We thought of him as a human domestic appliance. For Markus, most impossible things became possible. He could repair broken oil lamps, knot rope ladders, prepare mousetraps, mix rat poison, sharpen knives to hair-thick sharpness, and block up mouse-holes. He could spin anecdotes, make fireworks, carve puppets, and perform little plays. In short, Markus could do everything. If something was needed in the household, an essential tool, an ax or saw gone astray, Markus would fetch it. Markus was especially wonderful because he could fix my toys and dolls and because he knew wonderful stories and would sometimes scare me with tales about talking bears and blue snakes that could cure illnesses by climbing through chimneys at night. One day, when I was helping in the kitchen, he frightened me by saying that, if I ate raw dough, I would fly away.

Markus was also honest and a stern moralist. As he got older, he became more and more eccentric and convinced that he was part proprietor of our estate. He shuffled around imperiously as if in a bourgeois straitjacket, acted like a walking book of rules and laws, and treated other help with the condescension that comes naturally to those who occupy a higher station in life. A solid, respectable citizen, he fancied himself a chip off the old Geller block. Every evening Markus stood in front of the stove, deep in thought, as he prepared borscht and kasha, cut bread and grated radishes, and lit the fire, all for himself. Surely, with the help of these devoted people, the Geller family and its treasured possessions would have no problem surviving the short war.

In the evenings, the family sat around the steaming samovar and worried more about saving the furs, linen, and silver than about digging a shelter in the root cellar. Where to hide the fur coats? Where to bury the silver? What about Sonia's dowry? What about the scalloped candy dishes? Where to store the beautiful, starched and sparkling linens for future holiday celebrations? Grandmother and Aunt Sonia got very busy with the linen inventory. Sonia had a special notebook and, as Grandmother counted, she recorded the tablecloths, napkins, hand-embroidered doilies, tea towels, and cushion covers that needed to be saved. The stuff was loaded into a dresser case and locked. Marfa was entrusted with the keys to the fine linens and bedding; she jangled the heavy metal hoop of keys with great authority. This was serious and secretive business, done behind the heavy closed wooden doors of the dining room, without the knowledge of any other household help.

I was happy and felt important to be included in the effort. The samovar hummed and splattered. Every few minutes, another member of our brigade would rest at the table and drink strong tea with sugar. When Marfa was finished with her dresser case, she was thanked and dismissed, while my grandmother and Sonia continued with the more serious silver inventory. That work was occasionally interrupted when all the women disappeared into the bedroom to sew gold coins and jewelry into their brassieres and corsets.

Back in the dining room, large, dark, groaning cupboards, smelling of wax polish, were opened, pouring out heavy silverware and filigreed spice boxes in the shape of towers and steeples, Meissen plates, crystal vases, old books, large and small serving platters, dainty candy dishes, silverware, and all kinds of silver serving utensils. As the treasures were laid out, counted, and packed into two large tin bath tubs to be buried deep in the cherry orchard, I wandered about, adding something of my own to the collection. What about my toys, books, puppets, and dolls? I thought about this carefully and decided to slip my most beautiful Shirley Temple porcelain doll into the tin tub packed with silver. That was my own undercover contribution to the war effort. My uncle, father, and Markus carried out the secret mission that night and nothing about the tin tubs or their location was ever mentioned again.

Next came the fur coat operation. The men's heavy fur coats were a problem. So were a few special umbrellas with gold or ivory handles, as they were stiff and difficult to pack. My favorite furs belonged to my grandfather. One was an elegant beaver and sealskin coat, inherited by my father; the other a huge red fox coat inherited by Uncle Schloyme. For me, the red fox coat seemed to have a life of its own even though its old master was dead. I imagined the coat's sleeves as paws and the round collar as a mouth, and was convinced the coat was smiling at me, saying that everything was going to be alright, that the family and our possessions would be safe. My mother's furs reassured me even more. Romance, excitement, and the sweetest scents emanated from her karakul coat. It was mysterious, marvelous, curly, and warm. Spring lived in that coat, which had a rare silky and slippery lining embroidered with lilies of the valley in deep purple on a lilac background. It smelled of perfume and love, and as I covered myself with it again, I dreamed of living in it forever. With rubber galoshes on my feet shining like patent leather, and a muff on my hands, I could go anywhere and always be ready for life's next adventure! Mother wanted to give her old squirrel coat to Marfa, but Aunt Sonia advised against it, just in case we had to stay in Zloczów over the winter.

I crept out and sadly piled it together with the other coats. The bulky fur mountain was reflected in the mirror of a mighty wardrobe, but when no one was looking, I hid again under that mound of coats, feeling safe and warm. Before mother was ready to wrap her furs in rustling tissue paper and put them to sleep in moth balls on top of the men's furs in a trunk filled with camphor and cedar, I wriggled out again, disappointed that no one was paying attention to my games.

All possessions were finally hidden—some buried in the earth, some in corsets, others in the wooden shack where potatoes and bee-keeping equipment were stacked for the winter. Our family packed trunks and valises, and, with Olga in charge, we left for Zloczów, never again to see Tomasz, Marfa, Maryla, Markus, the house, the magic radio, the egg-yellow bench in the yard, or my father's family.

6

GRANDFATHER MENDEL

MY GRANDFATHER IN ZŁOCZÓW
was full of fun and mischief. He was jolly and handsome. His
hair and short, pointy beard were dark and curly, and he
smelled more of strong alkaline soap than cologne. He was a
friendly man, full of tales and jokes, forever pinching and
kissing my grandmother, Chana. I could tell that made her
feel loved and special. He also bought treats and surprises for
his grandchildren and doted on my mother as his special
princess.

Descended from a family of merchants and tavern keepers, he had three brothers who owned government monopo-
lies related to food and drink. Mendel's business rested on a

state monopoly license for selling grain, paper, and tobacco to
the army. He was proud of his business, proud to be a citizen
of the big, colorful Austro-Hungarian Empire and a subject
of Franz Joseph, whose old portrait hung in his warehouse.
He was savvy and generous, a rabbi, politician, lawyer, and
banker for the Jewish community of Złoczów all rolled into
one. For Grandfather Mendel, business was always good.
The Jewish business people and local population had to
remain flexible and pragmatic regardless of how wars, annex-
ations, and pogroms changed life and politics.

I myself heard him say, "If I have to help, I always give
with warm hands." Everyone in the little town knew Mendel,
and when I walked in the street with Olga, people would stop
and say, "Oh, you are Mendel's granddaughter! What a little
beauty!"

Złoczów had two main streets, which met in the *rynek*.
The old market square was in business twice a week. On one
corner was the new cinema, followed by a café, the *kawiarnia*,
a town park with tall chestnut trees, and a government building housing the post office and the police station. One street
had many shops, a printing establishment, and a factory that
assembled paper boxes and containers. Mendel's granary and
the warehouse that supplied food for the armies stationed in

Galicia were located in the other, more commercial street. In the summer, the church bells clanged, the larks trilled, and the crickets chirped without letup.

Złoczów's middle class lived in an almost unbroken façade of two-story apartment buildings with wrought-iron balconies. Most of the side roads were unpaved tracks, muddy in winter and dusty in summer. The railroad station was at the end of town. The train brought few travelers and only stopped three times a week. Beyond the station, the street turned into a hilly, dusty road that ran to the cemetery and the prison, an old castle or *Schloss*. Surrounding the town were wide, flat plains that extended as far as the eye could see, occasionally interrupted by gentle hills crisscrossed by rivers and pools, dappled with marshes and forests. The silence of the fields was only occasionally broken by the howl of locomotives.

Złoczów was a garrison town and, thus, a merry place. Soldiers in colorful uniforms of blue, red, and black, with gold epaulets, strolled through the park, where a military band played every Sunday. The *kawiarnia*, still decorated with Habsburg flags, double eagles, and banners, was the center of action. Mundek, the old waiter, usually spotted my grandfather and brought him the proper cherry *schnapps*. Złoczów was also one of the centers of Jewish Enlightenment, the *Haskala*.

Uncle Izio, Mendel's older brother, owned a brewery and a soda-bottling factory. His deliverymen, dressed in colorful vests and hats, drove the horse-drawn wagons filled with boxes of siphon bottles containing seltzer water. The clanging of the bottles on the rough dirt roads resembled bells and brought customers out of their houses.

Another brother, Uncle Fischl-Schmiel, was famous in the province for his rowdy tavern and blacksmith shop, where horses were changed for long-distance travel. The inns and taverns were short distances from the town. They were especially popular, as liquor in Złoczów was more expensive and subject to extra taxes. The Jewish tavern keepers had the license to sell alcohol to peasant *muzhiki* who would drink, eat, and have their fights and arguments. Once a month, nattily turned out and looking like a minor diplomat, Mendel entertained the sergeant of the *gendarmerie* and his cronies at the Kasztanka tavern in the village of Podhorce. Mendel wore a brown suit and bowler hat and sported a gold chain that emerged from his buttonhole, looped across his belly, and disappeared into a pocket. Each time he greeted his guests with laughter and mild surprise as they sat down around a wooden table to drink schnapps or sip coffee and tea from decorated cups.

The district had thirteen policemen and five officials who lived off bribes because no one paid taxes. Trivial crimes were not investigated, arson was considered an act of personal retribution and overlooked, and manslaughter was viewed as the effect of excessive alcohol consumption. No one paid attention to the counterfeiters. All in all, however, the town and countryside were suffused with a quiet serenity.

Certain holidays, like Christmas, Epiphany, and Shrove Tuesday, were special in *Złoczów*. Too much vodka and boredom soon turned into brawls. Two teams, each representing half the *town*, faced each other on the meadow near the church. It was against the rules to use anything but fists. Adults, adolescents, and old men all took part. Each partner selected an opponent equal to himself in age and size, and the whole place turned out to watch. Some peasants needed a few drinks to bolster their courage. Uncle Fischl-Schmiel then came to the rescue. The tavern was just down the road from the church, and all kinds of spirits were supplied for cash or credit.

These brawls fed into the virulent anti-Semitism in towns and villages. "The Jews take our money, make us drink, and then cause us to fight and insult our brother Slavs! Kill the Jews and save the Slavs!" But hatred and resentment of Jews had less to do with religion than with class and status. Since it was rare for Poles or Ukrainians to be in business, Jews were their primary contact with the incomprehensible and mysterious world of money. The Jews weren't liked because even, if honorable and helpful, they were held responsible for imposing financial pain on the villagers.

My grandfather and mother were active Zionists. She had been a member of the Zionist group at the gymnasium in Złoczów and the University of Lwów, which had a tiny quota of Jewish students who had to sit on ghetto benches in back of the classroom.

Many young Zionists went to the deserts of Palestine to escape violent anti-Semitism and work the land, but my grandparents would have never allowed their only child to go to a distant country, where riots and disturbances were commonplace and the future uncertain. The Levant, Palestine, seemed too Asiatic, too primitive, and too backward, lacking in any standards of hygiene or culture. My mother had to satisfy the Zionist passion that throbbed in her heart by reading Zionist poetry and naming me Shoshana, the Hebrew translation of my great-grandmother's name, Rose.

When the Russian tanks arrived, in September 1939,

everything changed. The Jews heaved a sigh of relief, and some thought the war was over. The Russian soldiers marched through the town all day long, singing songs, with children running after them. Russian music blared from the park; red banners with the hammer and sickle were strung across the town square. Stores were opened and they filled up with Russians. The Bolsheviks paid high prices for shoes and clothes, and would pay any amount for watches.

Soon businesses and factories were requisitioned, and before long my grandfather's warehouse was owned by the proletariat and guarded by Russian troops. But since the warehouse supplied flour, salt, and other commodities to the entire Red Army in our district, he was appointed *upravlyayushchii* (boss), and the new powers didn't interfere with his authority. He was very crafty in protecting his workers from this workers' government.

But what good was being the boss without being in charge of your business? He went to work every day, but he no longer laughed or told funny stories when he came home. "Woe unto us. Where is the sweet Revolution?" he muttered. "The future is hopeless. The Revolution—the great light in the East—promised happiness, but it brings chaos."

One evening he returned in a panic, saying that the army

had taken delivery of a huge consignment of corn that was moldy with maggots. The delivery was his responsibility. The corn had come from his warehouse! A meeting had taken place in his warehouse, and he had been denounced and declared an enemy of the revolution, a class enemy. His workers tried to interfere. "You are not to touch him! Not even one hair on his head! *Pan Zwerling, vin nash bat'ko,*" one Ukrainian had even shouted. "Mister Zwerling is our father!"

One morning, men in army uniforms and the Soviet secret police, the NKVD, came to arrest him. My grandmother and mother argued, pleaded, and cried with the officials. My grandfather's face turned red and purple. He stared at one of the commissars in disbelief. He and other class enemies were being sent off to work in Archangelsk in Siberia.

What was happening, and why? He was being arrested for being a *burzhuy* and *spekulant*, a bourgeois speculator and profiteer—in short, a traitor. He was accused of selling sacks of flour on the side, instead of giving them to the people. That same day, a group of shopkeepers with Grandfather Mendel among them was collected at the railroad station. That night, they were deported east, to Russia.

The family was inconsolable. We all hoped that it was a terrible mistake. I was told that he would surely be back, any day. My grandmother and mother visited different offices, carrying lots of documents, while I tried to help by searching for him with Olga at the train station, the town square, the warehouse, and his brother's tavern. The family waited for news. I was five, and his disappearance was my second loss in one year. I understood Grandfather Jacob's illness and death, and the funeral. I knew about cemeteries and dead people. But this grandpa had pink cheeks and was healthy, friendly, and a lot of fun. Why had the same Russians who gave us candy and played accordions taken him away?

Although Olga was also upset, she used the occasion to engage in further lessons about the Jewish people. She said they were cruel and greedy. Grandfather wanted to make money and had not believed in Jesus, who said that the meek shall inherit the earth. Although Communists also did not believe in Jesus, they did believe in helping the poor. She said Grandfather Mendel had been arrested because he handled money every day. She said she hated Jews, both because they crucified Christ and because they liked money so much. Other Jews were working for Russians, and for world revolution. She knew for a fact that two of the commissars were Jews from Kiev, and a third, Kaganovich, was a big Communist boss. Olga also hated the Russians because the soldiers were vulgar; they had no manners, spitting, farting, grabbing, and demanding. The women were laughable; they waltzed around town in nightgowns, thinking they were the height of bourgeois fashion, and none attended church.

Soviet power had arrived in Złoczów, but there were debates and arguments over how long that power would stay. Olga said that Russia, like Rome, would go down in flames. Soon the Germans and the Ukrainians would set things right in this topsy-turvy world. Too bad my hair was not flaxen colored. But if I behaved properly, said the catechism, and atoned for all my sins, the nuns who lived in the great big cloister would save me until the war ended and we got back to Włodzimierz. She embroidered her stories in the language of fairy tales, which I truly believed.

Nuns would save me with their prayers, and I would walk with them, the brides of Christ, in eternal bliss. When the time was right, silken ladders guided by angels in heaven would swing from Złoczów to Włodzimierz and take us back home to be among the blessed, to play with my dear friends in the meadows or in the cemetery.

Meanwhile, Olga and I continued searching for Grandfather. She was sure that the railroad station was where he would reappear.

On the days the trains ran, the station bustled with Russian soldiers and families with suitcases, sacks, trunks, and children. Passengers paced nervously along the platform. The arrival of the stationmaster was ceremonious and exciting for me. It meant that, after a long time waiting, something would happen soon. His bright red cap glistened in the sun, and his shiny metal whistle sparkled.

The train pulled into the station, its brakes pouring off steam. The sound of the conductor's whistle sent a shiver down my spine and kindled a little flame in my chest.

Grandfather Mendel is coming! This time for sure! I was absolutely certain as I pulled on Olga's dress. I carefully studied all the disembarking passengers' faces. Each time a new face appeared, I felt waves of excitement and distress.

I could feel myself jumping into his strong arms. His tickling beard would kiss my face as he reached deep into his pockets to stuff a marzipan treat into my mouth. I tugged on Olga's dress, jumped up and down, and could not contain my excitement. "He's arrived! He's getting off right now, this time for sure!"

But he never showed up. The crowd got smaller and smaller, people left, and only the passengers who were boarding remained.

The air grew calm, and the sun poured down, making the dust glisten. At the last sound of the stationmaster's whistle, the train gave another start and slowly moved off. All hope of Mendel's return was lost again.

7
GOING TO
THE MOVIES

WHEN THE WAR BEGAN, we moved to
my grandmother's house in Zloczów. Olga came with us.
Leaving Wlodzimierz was difficult for her. She was cranky
and irritable most of the time, though a little more upbeat
after the Germans attacked Russia and overran the town in
June 1941. Olga said that they had come to liberate Ukraine,
promising a free Ukraine without Russians, Poles, and Jews.

The Christian population of Zloczów came out to greet
the German soldiers. Well-dressed warriors on lorries, jeeps,
and motorcycles, field glasses and whistles hanging from their
necks, boots gleaming—they were a welcome change from
the shabby Russians. Girls in native Ukrainian costumes

came with salt and bread and flowers. Olga put me on her shoulders to watch them, but Grandmother was cautious and, after a short time, forbade me to go out with Olga. Olga was happy to have the Russians gone. "Don't worry. The Germans will rescue our native land. They will destroy communism and make us independent again! Ukraine will be free, hurrah!" Meanwhile she spent lots of time at the Ukrainian church, where she knew people from her old village and met new friends. She told us she had joined the Khmelnytsky Club, a religious patriotic group, and was now a serious Ukrainian patriot. Her nanny duties became perfunctory. Babcia Hancia mostly watched me play on the balcony as Olga went to her church meetings.

I was happy with the arrangement and sometimes played with my grandmother, glad that the curved cast iron spokes of the balcony shielded me from the street below, where German soldiers strutted around the little park. Their boots and caps glistened in the sun, while the huge, short-haired, well-groomed German shepherds, with enormous white teeth, trotted along. These soldiers were different from the Russians. The Russians were friendly, laughed a lot, sang and played accordions, and always gave me lumps of sugar or sweets, and I missed them. I couldn't understand the fuss.

We were no longer important people in this town, no one knew us, and people only paid attention to the German soldiers and the Ukrainian police.

One day Olga returned from town, very excited, to announce that the new cinema in town would reopen for evenings and matinees. Named *Uciecha* (Pleasure), it had been completed the year the war began. The German commander in charge had decided to open its doors again because entertainment and culture were necessary for military morale in the provinces.

A small-scale version of the Lwów Opera House, the Uciecha boasted a white stucco pleasure dome, columns and muses, and two regal stone lions at the front door. It had been built and operated by Mr. Golubczyk, a Jewish draper, an energetic and enterprising man who fancied himself a member of the avant-garde and worked on Sundays showing films. The drapery shop was now defunct, and he was content to have his daughter manage the few women sewing German uniforms. He was interested in all things technical and artistic about movie making and loved the movie business. He ran his films both for the "glory" of the Soviet Union and of the Reich. Alas, the timing of his investment was not opportune. The opening of the cinema coincided with the outbreak of war, and poor Mr. Golubczyk had to operate the business in wartime. But his love of art, and his need of approval by the authorities, motivated him to supervise and manage the theater, even after the Russians expropriated his shop and factory and exiled his son to Siberia.

Mr. Golubczyk was a jolly man. His legs were short and knock-kneed, his hairless skull was smooth as a billiard ball, and his handlebar mustache glistened with pomade. On Sunday afternoons, come rain or shine, dressed in a brown velvet jacket scented with a discreet hint of lilac, a boutonniere, and a sparkling cravat, he stood in front of the movie house, welcoming the locals as well as the Gestapo.

There was sadness in his eyes, but his shiny pink face continued to smile as he greeted people. With dignity and humor, his sparkling eyes and constantly moving curled mustache hinted at the great magic and mystery soon to flow from the screen.

I had to promise to be extraordinarily well behaved there, just as if we were on an outing in Wlodzimierz, where people knew us. The interior of the cinema was more beautiful than the façade. Burgundy velvet curtains and two pink marble statues flanked the stage. The deep seats were soft, plush burgundy velvet, and on special occasions a piano player also performed to the left of the stage. I buried myself in that magical kingdom as I sat and waited in the dark for the film to begin. When it did, I had to lift the seat and sit on the ledge to see the screen.

Olga explained that the cinema was a very special place. When the velvet curtain opened, magic would begin. Soon real people, in black and white, would appear and speak to each other, while beautiful music enveloped the theater. The actors in the movie told a story, just like the stories in fairy tales and other books Olga and I read, but the stories we saw in the cinema were more like real life. People could be passionate, dramatic, and romantic. When I didn't understand, she explained about love: about holding each other, kissing, crying, laughing, smiling, and arguing, all at different times. I was too young to appreciate the dramatic quality of the cinema. The stories were meant for older, more sophisticated brains than mine. I remember nothing but startling adventures of strange heroes and heroines, violent catastrophes, beautiful maidens abducted by cruel Cossacks, a wicked people who poisoned and stabbed each other in furious or jealous rages, and all manner of unheard-of things in a strange world.

Then, one Sunday afternoon, Olga vanished. The cine-

ma felt especially warm and safe that day; the music was wonderful with the promise of an especially arresting fairy tale
romance. When the movie ended, we put on our coats and
walked out to the little *kawiarnia* next door. We savored the
fresh strawberry ice cream, eating very slowly and thought-
fully, and listened to the chiming of little spoons against the
glass bowls. My knees were pressed together against the low
marble table, as we sat in our little nook. It was early autumn.
A noiseless rain was watering the trees on the town square
and sweeping small yellow leaves into puddles. For me, the
movie magic continued. Chestnuts finished blooming, and
the wet branches of trees looked like bent paws holding tall
white flowers.

Olga and I had a long discussion about the plot of the
movie, especially about Magda, the lady with the beautiful
huge eyes and tiny lips who ran away with her lover. It made
me feel very grown up. I think that was the first time that she
didn't order me around and treated me as a friend. I actually liked her. I almost loved her when she handed me an extra
favorite treat, a marzipan piglet wrapped in pink cellophane,
and told me to wait for her in the shop while she ran a short
errand. She was kinder than usual when she gave me the
piglet. She then left the shop and turned the corner in front

of the square, promising to return before I finished the treat. I waited for her, watched the people and the rain, ate my piglet very slowly, and waited some more. Suddenly, I felt terribly afraid that I was alone. Where was Olga? Where could she have gone for so long? She was not one of the people on the screen who disappear at the end with the music. She was my nanny and sometimes my friend. I almost loved her that afternoon, and she belonged to me. Although I was frightened, I did not cry but looked serious and intent, like a grown-up with business to do. I tried desperately to block my rising anxiety by remembering the film. After all, Magda had been in great danger, and her lover had returned and rescued her. My business was to figure out how to get home as quickly as possible.

It was getting dark. A hanging sign creaked in the wind, and the clouds in the sky became more violet. From the shop, I recognized a man who worked in my grandfather's warehouse. He was talking to a soldier. Nonchalantly, I put on my coat, skipped over, and told him that Olga had never returned from her errand, that I couldn't find her. He took my hand, and we began our walk to Babcia Hancia's house.

The family was panic-stricken by the time the man and I climbed up the beautiful cast iron staircase. Why were we so very late? There were soldiers in the street! It was almost dark! My grandmother was shouting, and my mother began hitting me. They were very frightened, and I was to blame. My grandfather had just vanished a short time before, and now this!

The commotion, along with the relief, lasted a while before they realized that Olga was still missing. Where was she? I did not know. She had left me waiting in the *kawiarnia* and never returned. She had vanished, but it was not my fault. Later my mother explained that she had run away because she was in love with a handsome Ukrainian soldier from the Khmelnytsky Club, who took her with him to fight the Russians.

Months later, cold November rains and winds deluged Zloczów. Even the stone lions in front of the Uciecha looked sad: the place had been shut down and Mr. Golubczyk was taken away to the forest in another *Aktion*. But Babcia Hancia told me not to worry. Mr. Golubczyk's velvet jacket was in safekeeping with Pavel, the movie custodian, and perhaps he would return from the forest and open the movie house again. Maybe Olga would also return from the forest. Why, I wondered, were so many people going to the forests?

If she didn't return, then surely Grandpa Mendel would

come home, and I would be able to go to the cinema with
him!

8
BURIED ALIVE

"**T**HERE WAS A MASS EXECUTION in the forest of Jelechowice," our cousin Pipa told my grandmother after he returned to her house in Zloczów. He was caked in mud, wearing a sack and stinking of death. I took special notice of the black slime between his toes.

"They brought us from the work camp by lorry, and we had to dig our graves a day before the shootings. The Ukrainian police put a wide plank across the pit where we were told to undress. They were drunk. They used only one bullet per victim. Many were buried alive, just a thin layer of earth over them. I was buried with the others, but I wasn't even wounded. Somehow, the bullet missed me, and I jumped into the pit. The moon was round. The night was full of distant and painful cries. I decided to get out and run, while the bloody earth on the pit was still moving."

Pipa was my favorite relative from Wlodzimierz. He had introduced me to the village boys, and sometimes I'd been lucky enough to be included in their games and mischief. Destiny had chosen him to be admitted to Lwów University on the tiny Jewish quota, and he provided much *naches* for his parents, grandparents, and family. When the first bombs fell on Lwów in September 1939, Pipa was a nineteen-year-old university student.

I have a photo postcard of him with his father. Pipa is about sixteen on the card. Uncle Schloyme has a pair of binoculars with Zeiss lenses slung over his neck. He and Pipa are carrying a deer, strung upside down by its legs to a pole. Propped on a bench is a gun case; nearby are two ammunition boxes. My father said they were of brown leather, polished to look like hard wood. It is clear that the photograph was an emblem of privilege, taken to impress family members in Europe and America.

My father used to tell stories of their hunting, a sport reserved for *goyim*. Pipa was a very good sportsman, a good horse rider, and physically strong. He thought of himself as a child of nature and loved the wild forests and countryside. He did very well in sports competitions, so his friends in gymnasium couldn't say, "Oh, he's a Jew. He's not good enough." He used to show off his marksmanship. My father once told a story of how, on a summer day, Pipa riddled a rusty "No Hunting" sign in the woods with bullets—a daring feat unheard of for a Jew.

When the Germans entered Lwów in 1941, he was rounded up with other Jewish students and taken to a work camp near Brody, where he slaved building a road. We hadn't heard from him for many months, until that very early morning when he appeared. I was eating breakfast when I heard my grandmother's terrible gasp, her crying to God for help. I jumped up and saw him, a boy come back from the dead.

After his escape from Jelechowice, he had hid in a cabbage field. "Blackness and fear filled me. There was muck in my skin and hair. I felt clammy and cold, dripping and dirty. I stayed where I was. I wanted to sink into the field. I took a stick and dug, planting myself like a turnip, hiding my face with cabbage leaves, and lying there, invisible. I dreamt of bread. When I awoke, my jaw was sore from chewing air. I awoke in the milky dawn sky, dim with hunger, and imagined placing tiny pieces of bread that tasted like chocolate into my mouth. But the piercing hunger wouldn't leave, and I had to move."

Pipa didn't know how to get to Zloczów. The shadows of the telegraph poles along a railway line showed him which way was north. He was also able to use trees for direction, because moss grows on the north side of trunks. Finally, he reached our house in the ghetto. But escaping death was not enough for him. He felt like a caged animal in our house. He spent his time slurping soup and porridge at the kitchen table. When he wasn't eating, he was sleeping, arms outstretched, breathing heavily. His sleep was deep, troubled, but dreamless.

As the days went on, he slept less and fidgeted more. Each morning, before my father went to work for the *Wehrmacht*, Pipa told him he would run away from this "republic of fear and terror" and join the partisans in the forest near Bryansk.

Rumors of German determination to make Galicia *Judenrein*—free of Jews—abounded in the ghetto. My mother and grandmother were busy with plans for financing the bunker under the barn at Demko's farm, where we were going on "vacation." The village of Podhorce was close, and for me there was the promise of a fun ride on the hay wagon. Weeks passed. It was almost time for the hayride. Mother and Grandmother pleaded with Pipa to come with us. He refused. He said that the forest and the partisans were his next university.

"Compared with the ghetto, it will be heaven. In the woods, among the pine and fir trees, I will be free."

Pipa bartered my father's watch for a handgun and, pale and frightened, escaped on a lorry, hiding among sacks of flour. We knew that Hitler had sent his most ferocious and lawless troops into the dense forests with orders to kill all partisans. We never heard from Pipa again.

9
ZOSIA SLONIMSKA

BABCIA'S LARGE APARTMENT was in the ghetto, so we didn't have to move, but one day, frightened strangers with panicked faces hurriedly carried furniture, pots, pans and mattresses up the stairs. Four people and three unkempt, disheveled children came to live with us. I was glad that Olga was gone. She would surely have been upset by the commotion. My world was turning topsy-turvy.

Who were these people? Why were they coming to live with us? I hated the idea of sharing Babcia's home, which now was also my house. I stood in the doorway, mouth set, squinting and angry. I pinched and pushed the smallest of the children, and wished I had big growling dogs, like the

Germans, to halt the commotion in our hallway.

My brother Janek was also curious, but he continued playing with his toys and occasionally threw blocks at the moving mattresses. My mother explained that the Germans had ordered local Jews living in the ghetto to take other displaced Jews into their houses and apartments. She said these other Jews had been chased out of their houses and had no place to live, and that we had to follow the orders of our "wartime masters." Anyway, I would be leaving soon for a vacation with a Gentile family, the Slonimskis.

That Sunday afternoon we found a droshky to take us to my new family. The weather was fine, the sky a bright grayish blue. We drove in the direction of the river and pulled up alongside a grassy embankment. Below us stretched the river, winding toward meadows. Dark clumps of river weeds and wildflowers softened the edges of the banks. The tranquil water flowed by as we pulled over to a shady spot to eat our white-bread-and-butter sandwiches with hard-boiled eggs. I felt that my mother and I were on an endless, tranquil holiday, away from the hysteria of the ghetto.

Our droshky passed an orchard laden with bright red apples. Flocks of geese pecked at a green slope. I saw thatch-roofed cottages and clumps of birch trees. I knew that I was going to strangers, but, too frightened to face reality, I wanted to believe that I was living a fairy tale. When we neared the farmyard pond, the road bent up the hill to the Slonimski house. It was painted green and white, with a gabled roof and a big red chimney. Unlike the surrounding tumble-down cottages with unkempt thatched roofs, it was large and important.

My fairy tale ended when we pulled up to the courtyard. I was given a new name—Zosia Slonimska—and I was to be a cousin visiting the family. The Slonimskis were nice. They were a miller's family. Mr. Slonimski was a business associate of my grandfather, Mendel, and Maria, my new "aunt," seemed kind but anxious as she nervously patted my head, shoulders, or hands.

My mother and grandmother gave me strict instructions about how to behave. Their instructions were different from, and much more serious than, Olga's. I understood that I had to behave exactly as they said. My life depended on it. It was a matter of life or death. My mother hung a crucifix on my neck, and my grandmother cried and, from time to time, invoked Churchill's name for help. Olga would have been proud to see me wearing the crucifix. I too hoped that the cross and my new Polish name would save me, and that the cross would point to the velvet rope in heaven where angels frolicked.

I wasn't allowed to cry. Mother's blue eyes spoke of fear and danger even as she smiled and left after placing another one of my favorite dolls on my new bed. She kissed me and promised to visit every Sunday afternoon.

Real, unrelenting anxiety had begun for the neatly dressed and pigtailed Zosia, who had come to live with the Slonimskis. I invoked Olga's name for help, and remembered that walking very straight, as if with a broom between my shoulders, would make me look even less Jewish. My mother's eyes had offered no assurances. She didn't love me and was abandoning me, I thought. I was afraid of being lost and cast away, terrified that, after she left, I was never going to see her again.

She came to visit many times, and our visits were very quiet. I was old enough to be a "good little girl." Each time she came to visit felt as if it was her last.

Being in new surroundings, with a strange new family, was difficult. I missed everybody. I was very serious and careful and polite with strangers. It was easier to make friends with chickens, ducks, and geese. The chicken house was a special source of comfort, and I inspected the nests every day for new eggs. Somehow, the warm eggshells gave me comfort and safety in that unfamiliar world. When bored with chickens and geese, I moved to the front garden where I spent many hours playing house with the grasses and flowers. My tranquil and playful world of Wlodzimierz was gone, but the bright sunshine, white clouds, fragrant blossoms on apple and cherry trees, and the sounds of house animals provided a peaceful, if fleeting, respite from anxiety. I decided to make flower wreaths for my hair, to go with the crucifix. I tried to remember the catechism and the prayers Olga taught me for church, and would recite them to myself. My new family, and Olga, would be proud of me in my new identity, and surely I would attain salvation for my family.

One day, as I was playing in the yard, a German soldier, spotlessly dressed in a perfect uniform, shiny hat, and polished boots that glistened like mirrors came up the dusty road to the house. With him was a large, well-groomed German Shepherd. I had always been afraid of dogs and especially terrified of German Shepherds. I noticed them always beside important officers in the parks and squares of Zloczów.

The soldier entered the house with his dog. He was handsome. His face smelled of my father's cologne. He put me on his lap with a playful smile, and started bouncing me on his knees. I glanced at my own dusty sandals and wondered how his boots had missed all the mud and dust on the road. The dog sat quietly beside him. Its open mouth and perfect, sharp white teeth made it look like it was smiling. Although my knees shook when its body came close to my legs, I was beginning to feel more at ease, somehow safe on the handsome man's lap. I liked the bouncing and wanted to stay there.

"What a pretty dress you have, and what beautiful curly hair. What is your name?"

"Zosia," I said, "and I am six years old."

"Where do you come from, and where are your mommy and daddy?"

"I live here with my aunt, Maria. My parents are working in Germany."

"What a pretty child you are, and so smart."

The soldier bounced me off his knees as he spoke and said he would have to take me with him. "We will go to the old castle near town to play with some other nice children."

The dog also began moving around and quietly growling. I was terrified and found it hard to breathe. My head shook as my neck went into a spasm, which continued as a painful reflex long after the war. I felt helpless and alone, and much more fearful than I did while waiting alone at the *kawiarnia* for Olga months before. There was nothing I could do when "Aunt Maria" packed my little brown suitcase with toys, books, and the doll. Holding the soldier's hand, I walked down the road to the army car. A man I recognized from my grandfather's warehouse was now working as a chauffeur for the Germans. The car bumped along the dirt road, its wheels turning up clouds of dust. I tightened my face, and shivers went down my back. The dog was sitting next to me, his open mouth still seemed to be smiling. The driver announced that we were going to the Zamek.

The Zamek—the *Schloss*, or castle—was familiar to me. I used to play around the big stone fortress on many summer visits to Zloczów. We had amused ourselves by going to the beach or the Zamek. The "beach" was a strip of riverbank painstakingly covered each season with a thick layer of white sand. An entrance fee made the beach exclusive and entitled visitors to the comfort of deck chairs, parasols, and changing cabins. Only the more intrepid swimmers braved the Zloczówka's swift currents, using a face-out-of-water style of breast stroke. Men, women, and children wore white rubber bonnets. Olga and I also put on white rubber shoes like ballet slippers to protect our feet from pebbles and the slimy feel of the bottom. By the time I was four, Olga was teaching me to swim.

When we didn't go to the river, there were outings into the forest. Often, returning to my grandmother's house, our hay cart would stop to rest at the Zamek.

The castle was very big and very old. Its massive walls were made of roughly hewn stones haphazardly dotted with small barred windows, smaller than the stones in the walls. The place was wild and mysterious. Grasses and moss covered its shady places. Wild poppies and cornflowers had long since overrun the neglected gardens. The castle was magical to me, and I loved stopping there. It was a great place to run around in. We played hide-and-seek in the dark and damp halls, and were happy to be "found" safe and happy outside. When the sun shone and the earth was warm, a wondrous calm, straight out of my fairy tale books, descended over it. Often we took out our nets and tried to catch butterflies.

Olga explained that, a long time ago, very rich and important people who ruled Zloczów had lived there. Many wars had been fought over the castle, but finally they had abandoned the place, and it had become a prison. The old rulers spoke German, and that's why it was called the *Schloss*. Olga never missed an opportunity for another carrot-and-stick sermon. She warned me that I, too, could be locked up if I behaved badly, and especially if I continued to pick my nose. That warning was coming true! I was terrified when the driver stopped the car at the rusty gates of the castle. I clutched the little suitcase for comfort, and prayed for the safety of my little doll, Marysia, who was hiding in the suitcase.

A woman in a dark uniform came to the car and took my hand. We walked into the castle and down a small, dark, damp stairway to a room with many cots, where she told me to leave the suitcase and my doll unprotected. I felt abandoned and helpless. I could not even cry. All I could do was breathe and look and listen. Children's voices drifted in from the courtyard. I walked to the little window and looked for familiar faces. I saw none. The children were being gathered for the noonday meal, and, not wanting to be alone, I walked down to the yard to be near them. The sun shone warmly and brightly. Only that morning, I had been in Aunt Maria's garden, where I'd made "garden salad" and chased the goats and chickens. Where was Aunt Maria? Where was my mother? Where were the mothers of the other children?

Suddenly, as I stood there, I thought I heard a clear bell go off near the castle gate. I listened again. It was not a bell but my mother's voice. I listened again to be sure it was real, and not like the voice of my grandfather I had imagined hearing at the railroad station. But no—again I heard her voice clearly, and saw her speaking to the guard at the gate. Mamusia had come to save me! It seemed she knew the guard, and their conversation was cordial. He let her in, and she ran to me with outstretched arms. Crying and shivering, she held me tight.

The news that I had been taken away from the Slonimskis had reached the family very quickly, and my grandmother had greased the proper palms to get my mother a work permit in the prison.

It was arranged with the director that she would work as a cook's helper in the prison kitchen and sleep in the tiny stone alcove nearby. I was only one of about two dozen children rounded up in the children's *Aktion* that day. Could it be one of Olga's miracles that my mother was now with me? Many Sundays had passed since I prayed in church with Olga, but with the Slonimskis, I was almost a Christian. That first sunny day in the castle was the longest, the most fearful, and the happiest day of my life. My mother had come to save me! Although we heard shouts, loud noises, and screams from other parts of the prison, I was no longer panic-stricken. I held on to my mother.

After the evening soup, the lady warden organized the children for their dormitory cots. It was time for me to go with them and unpack my little suitcase. "You will see your mama again tomorrow," she said.

My mother's face no longer glowed. She became agitated and nervous, held my hand very tightly, and would not let go. She smiled and pleaded with the other prison guard to allow me to sleep with her in the alcove. Her beautiful face, her sharp blue eyes, her body language—all begged that I sleep in her alcove. As their talk grew quiet and intimate, her face flushed and she smiled. The guard tapped her shoulder, also smiled, and said that he would return later. We both began to breathe more deeply, and I stopped trembling. As the other children were herded to their cots, my mother rocked me. I hid in her warm breasts and was happy.

Later that night, the guard returned. My mother covered me tightly with an extra straw mattress and said she would return soon. She had combed her hair, pinched her cheeks and quietly left with the guard. I waited. Through the tiny window up high, I could see the inky sky, bright stars, and the full moon. Some time later, my mother returned, smiled, and lay down on the cot beside me. The sultry aroma of her warm body made me happy. She smelled as familiar as warm milk, and I could feel the yielding softness of her breasts as she wept. Neither of us slept for a long time, and it was deadly quiet in the castle and in the courtyard. Suddenly, we heard steps, shouts, and screams, and then gunshots. The children's section was liquidated that night, and my little brown suitcase with all my storybooks disappeared. My beautiful Marysia was also lost! I could not save her.

I spent what seemed like endless days with my mother in the kitchen. I always stood very near her, following her movements as if attached by the same invisible velvet rope that held the angels together. I soundlessly followed her around as she peeled potatoes, chopped turnips or cabbage, and scrubbed pots. When she was able to rest, we sat close to the pale light of the window where I would sit in her lap, touching her warm breasts as she combed out my hair in her endless search for lice.

When she found one, out it came on her thumbnail, and she squashed it with her other thumb. I imagined that we were a monkey family, with the mother grooming her baby monkey as in one of the storybooks in my lost suitcase. I liked the crackling noise each time she found her prey. Sometimes I dozed on her lap as the offensive against the lice continued. She quietly told me how important it was for all the lice to be destroyed, because they carried a terrible sickness for people. She couldn't get any kerosene for washing my hair, and had to hunt and kill them herself. I listened carefully, but had trouble understanding how a little insect, which could be squashed so easily, had the power to kill.

She also told me stories about leaving the castle. If I continued to be good and very quiet, her new friend, "Uncle Staś," would help us get out in just a few more days. I could see my father, Babcia, and my brother Janek again! I imagined them all standing on our balcony, throwing candy and waving a welcome, as we had when the Russian troops came to Złoczów. But my mother said they would not be on the balcony. The Russian soldiers were no longer there, times were dangerous, little Janek cried a lot, and Babcia had taken him to relatives in a safer town. But I shouldn't worry. We would all be together again soon, because we were going on vacation to Demko's farm, where Demko was building a summer cottage for us. The place would be lots of fun, especially for me, because I could play with all the farm animals—cows, horses, sheep, and rabbits. I could chase the sheep with the other barefoot girls in the meadows, and maybe learn to ride a small horse. Demko's wife, Maronka, was famous for her delicious sugared cream, which we would eat with the juicy wild berries we could pick. She calmly told me stories about life on the farm, but her eyes and mouth spoke of worry and fear. Since it would take some time for the "cottage" to be ready, we would temporarily live in the attic while waiting for Babcia and Janek to arrive.

What an adventure, to sleep in the attic, I thought. Through the cracks of the roof, I could see the stars and the moon in the heavens. I was sure that, if I were especially good and quiet, I would even be able to see angels frolicking in the clouds. Mother agreed with me, and I wanted to believe every word she spoke.

10

HAYRIDE TO PODHORCE

IT WAS EARLY AUTUMN. The days were sparkling, sunny, and cloudless, with no autumn frost in the air. Autumn is the sweetest season in Poland, full of harvest smells and promise. But neither the season, nor the day, brought hope.

My father registered for work with the *Judenrat*, a council of elders who governed the ghetto for the Nazis, and was given a job as a draftsman for the German army, the *Wehrmacht*. He got up every morning, pale and frightened, washed and shaved, and got ready for work. His long, trembling fingers clutched a cigarette as he listened to the short-wave Grundig radio and gulped a glass of tea with milk.

When he wasn't smoking or drinking tea, he'd rub his forehead with his hands. Occasionally, he'd breathe out and mutter that life for us was "finished." It was the end. What did he mean? I knew the word "finish" was about finishing eating or other chores or games, but how could our life finish? It didn't make sense. I thought about Olga and life with the angels frolicking in clouds, and Jesus resurrected, and other paintings on ceilings of churches. My father was talking nonsense. He said good-bye to us each morning as if he were never returning, and then he would greet us after the day's work, ashen, pale, and gloomy. It seemed that each day signaled another reprieve for him and our small family. Each morning he walked to the town square, where a lorry picked up the workers for the civil engineering project. He was making maps of bridges and factories in the Zloczów area for the German military.

One afternoon, shots were fired in the inner courtyard of our apartment house, and a man was killed. I was not allowed to look out the kitchen window that faced the courtyard. My grandmother and mother assured me that nothing really bad had happened. The police had made a mistake and hurt a man who was now sleeping and resting because he was very tired from running. The family was frightened, and I was very curious and upset. Only my baby brother continued to build his block castles and then destroy them and throw the blocks around the room.

Finally I was able to get near the kitchen window and see the man. I was too frightened to look directly, so I squinted.

The man, wearing a somber black jacket, did indeed seem to be sleeping. His white, cold flesh was lifeless, his stiff body curled. Caked brown blood formed a thick stream from his nose to his chin. I knew he was dead because I had seen dead, stiff chickens and rabbits, and yet I kept wishing he would wake up, or at least that someone would take him away. But he didn't move. He lay in the same place for three days. I didn't want to believe he was dead. The body was near the courtyard fountain, the stench of death overwhelming. I was not allowed to walk to the fountain, and no one was organizing a funeral like the one we had for Grandfather Jacob in Wlodzimierz. Our life continued as if nothing had happened. "It is wartime, and unpleasant things happen," said Babcia Hancia, as she invoked Churchill's name again.

My mother also continued her routine of preparing and delivering hot lunches to my father. She had special permission from the Judenrat to deliver food to the German barracks and the office where he worked. Often, she also went to the village of Podhorce, where Grandfather Mendel's solid business connections and gold pieces were enabling her to plan our escape from Zloczów. She returned home very serious and frightened but always with a tense smile and hugs for us, along with two baskets filled with apples, plums, milk, eggs, and cheese for Babcia Hancia.

My mother never laughed nor sang again. Instead, she walked around the house in complete silence. I sensed big trouble and danger. She hugged and kissed us a lot. Still, mother's warm bosom felt like a nest, and I was the little bird. When she held me and rocked me, I remembered that same rocking from the terrible times in the castle.

Fear was in the air. Refugees told of murder, shootings, burnings, and the liquidation of ghettos in their little towns. The word *Judenrein* was whispered by everyone. I had no idea of what it meant. It wasn't a Ukrainian or Polish word, but somehow I knew it had to do with our family, the scary Germans and the Ukrainian police, and the dead man in our courtyard. Suddenly, the Ukrainian police started arresting Jews who were new in town and did not have documents. Babcia Hancia told me that the man asleep in our courtyard had been from another town and had gotten hurt because the police had chased him.

The barracks where my father worked for the Germans were part of an old factory on the outskirts of town, where the woods met the meadows far away from the Zloczów ghetto. The old factory had a new sign emblazoned on the entrance in German that read *Ein Volk, Ein Reich, Ein Führer* (One People, One Empire, One Leader). German officers who directed and supervised the Jews were also engineers. They were in charge, of course, but after some time, workers' faces grew familiar, and a relaxed camaraderie and trust grew between the Germans and their Jewish charges.

Lunch at the Gestapo headquarters was the high point of the day for the Germans. Precisely at one-thirty, a jeep rumbled down the dusty road to take the Germans to lunch. They left the small group of Jews on their own, whose relatives brought them food. Along with preparing the hot meals, my mother planned my father's escape. One morning, as I was eating porridge with islands of melted butter, she said that I would be allowed to go along with her on the hayride and visit my father.

She picked out several pieces of underwear and several dresses and told me to put them on, one on top of the other. Why the layers of clothes? Where were we really going in the hay wagon? I was old enough to do what she said: be very quiet and not ask questions.

That day, when the sun was high in the sky, Stefan—one of my grandfather's trusted peasants from Podhorce—and his hay wagon met us outside our courtyard. He loaded my mother's white enamel pails of food and drove us to the German barracks. She unloaded the pails and went to meet my father. Stefan dozed in the sunshine while I squirmed and sweated in layers of clothes and a bright, rose-covered peasant shawl. After lunch was over my mother walked my father over to the wagon and stuffed him under the fragrant hay. She climbed up next to us and covered both our heads with the shawl while Stefan's black whip nudged the horse slowly down the hot, dusty road to Demko's farm in the village of Podhorce. The little cart wobbled along until we made our way to the main road. Other horse-drawn peasant carts, piled high with hay, followed at a brisk trot, especially when the peasants cracked their whips.

The golden autumn sun warmed the farmers working the harvest in the flat, endless fields. The wheat was so tall that the shafts covered my head. At the edge of the horizon, I could see a line of trees that marked the boundary of the pastures to Podhorce.

A woman behind a rickety fence was scattering grain to

geese and chickens. As we passed fields and meadows, my mother held me closer and was less tense. "You were a good girl, just as I expected. Soon we will be having a vacation in the house Demko is building for us. Babcia Hancia and Janek are allready on vacation, in a different village. Soon they will come and live with us in our new house in Demko's farm."

I trembled with excitement and relief at the thought of picking berries, running in the meadows, and jumping bare-footed in real haystacks in Demko's fields.

By mid-1943, German bureaucrats were able to produce a statistical report with a satisfying zero. There was not one Jew left in Zloczów. The town had been made *Judenrein* (cleansed of Jews).

11
THE ATTIC

WHILE DEMKO WAS FINISHING our "summer cottage"—I didn't know then that it was really a bunker —we hid in the attic of the barn. The attic was very still. A shaft of sunlight gilded the dust on the barn window while I played games, waiting for specks of dust to change position. A splendid sunset lingered in the flamingo-pink sky, with long, dark violet, motionless clouds.

The days were boring and difficult. The action was out-side. Church bells clanged, larks trilled, and crickets chirped without letup. I knew that childhood was a meadow without borders or fences. Why was I sitting so still in the attic? I looked out on prickly, yellow fields and dreamed of running barefoot even if it hurt my feet. I wanted to be running with the farm girls chasing the cows. I dreamed of picking wild flowers and berries and collecting warm chicken eggs. If I couldn't be in the meadows, I wanted to wander free in the garden or sit on our big yellow bench at home, swinging my bare feet in the dust.

Nights in the attic were different. They were full of mystery. Five of us slept in the hayloft, warming each other. I was rocked gently in my mother's arms. Her warmth made me feel safe. The cracks in the roof of the barn let in a big sky, wondrous and full of sparkling stars. I was looking up at the house of God. How I wished to ride the stars to heaven where brides of Christ would welcome us to eternal bliss!

Every morning, Mother dressed and arranged her hair neatly, tidied our attic, and waited for our guests. Each day, we waited for the farm wagon with Babcia and Janek to roll up the hill to the barn. We waited for news, messages, and letters. Mother assured me that they were in a safe and friendly village, being well taken care of by Babcia's relatives, but that she had not been able to get word to us.

She continued to rock me and tell me what we'd do when they finally arrived. Janek would come just in time for the berry harvest. We would pick the best strawberries we could find, not the shy ones that grew around the barn, but the wild, luscious, juicy ones that stood proudly in clumps in the forest. Maronka, Demko's wife, would make delicious cream to mix with the juicy, crunchy wild berries. Our little family would be safe and together, the war would end very soon, and we would return to Wlodzimierz, where the boys, and surely Olga, were already waiting for us. I told Mother that, when Janek arrived, he could have my little stuffed bear, the only toy that had come with me in the hay wagon, and that Father would make a small wooden cart for the bear and Janek.

But the long summer stretched out, and there was still no news. Mother no longer waited for morning, nor did she fix her hair or tidy the attic with the little twig broom. She still told me stories about their imminent arrival, but she spoke in hushed and alarmed tones. She never smiled. Her face grew haggard, her eyes looked hurt, and her nervous fingers told a more tragic story.

She was consumed by the loneliness within her. Mother was desperate, losing hope, and very afraid, but she had to hold on to her dignity in front of me. It was only when I looked away that grief overcame her. When she glanced at my father, her panicked eyes pleaded for help. I also lost hope. At the same time I was too afraid to know what was really going on and therefore played along with her game.

One day Demko's brother, Stefan, and his wagon rolled up from Brody. Babcia and Janek did not come running to the barn. Instead, Stefan trudged over the hill and told my parents the story of their death. The Brody ghetto had been declared Judenrein two days after the Zloczów ghetto. The Ukrainian police had gathered up many older women and children, locked them in the synagogue, and set the building on fire. Stefan was sure that Babcia and Janek were among the victims, because his cousin Ivan, a Ukrainian policeman, said he had seen them in Brody the day before. Their deaths were kept a secret from me. Only my mother's silent and frightened eyes told the story I refused to accept. I continued to believe that they didn't die, that they were hiding somewhere, that we would look for them as soon as the war was over. To convince myself, I kept staring at mother, because surely, if something that horrible had happened, she would be crying. As my parents listened to Stefan, my father fidgeted with a vial of cyanide he had carried with him since rumors of the slaughter of Jews had begun. Stefan sat with us for awhile, bounced me on his lap, and gave me a lump of sugar. When he left, father looked at me for a long time and explained. "The Germans are liquidating the ghettos in all the towns. You must be very good and never make a sound."

I was proud that he was talking to me personally, that he had finally broken his silence and begun to explain everything as he had always done at home, especially now that I was so baffled.

"Papa," I said, "please tell me why we are here in the attic. What are 'ghettos'? What does the word 'liquidate' mean? Why did we leave our home and go into hiding? Why did I have to change my name? What does 'dangerous' mean?" I demanded an adult explanation for feelings I didn't want to understand.

He was still for a while, and then said sternly, "You must not ask. You must be silent. Our lives depend on your not giving us away."

How could their lives depend on me? Responsibility, and the gravity of his words, threw my neck into spasms again. My mother listened in agony, her body contorted, her face in despair, but I willed her not to cry, and she paid attention and didn't.

12
SLEEP

THE BUNKER WHERE WE HID for more
than a year had been dug beneath the cow shed by Demko
and his brother Stefan. The narrow rectangular space, which
reminded me of our vegetable cellar at home, was cold and
dark. The sides were damp earth, interspersed with patches
of mud and straw mixed like cement. The bunker stank of
old potatoes and rotten hay, of mushrooms and mold, and of
autumn forests in the rain. A heavy wooden plank served as
a trap door for the red-cheeked Demko to lower our food,
and bring up the excrement pail, every day. I could only tell
that day had come when the rooster started crowing and the
animals above began shuffling around and making noises.

Five of us hid in this gloomy cellar. There were, besides my parents and me, our cousin Buma and his girlfriend Donia, who had escaped from the ghetto. The two were in love. I wasn't quite sure what the word really meant, but I was jealous. To share a hiding place was as intimate a thing as I could possibly imagine. But they were devoted to each other and wouldn't let me enter their space. They only had each other, their families having been murdered in the Jelechowice forest. Again and again, in muffled tones, she told the story of finding her father's shirt and jacket on a truck returning from the killing fields. Buma and my mother tried to comfort her, but Donia cried and cried bitterly.

I tried to fathom the word "death" but couldn't. Now again, there was only a thin, fragile wall between the living and the dead. I knew it was something very terrible, because I had already seen the dead man in Grandmother's courtyard. I was scared by the very word. My mind connected it with terrible pain, even though my father explained to me that it was just an endless sleep.

I knew that no one was "dead" in our cellar. I believed that soon everything would change, and that nobody would ever die again. But my mother seemed desperate and frightened all the time. She rarely stroked my face, never smiled, and clutched me as if she were protecting me from death.

I understood that something terrible had happened to Babcia and Janek, but I did not permit myself to cry and had to remain brave. Crying was only for spoiled children. Crying was about not getting the treats or toys I wanted, about not being allowed to run around and play games with the boys in the cemetery. But why was Donia always crying about finding her father's clothes on the truck? I was confused. I certainly wished I could find some of the things that I had lost, like my fairytale books or the little doll in my suitcase. She should have been happy, I thought, to have found lost things.

The worst part of the cellar was the impenetrable darkness. How I wished to be in the barn attic again, where I could watch sun flecks in the meadows and clouds and stars at night. Sometimes, when it was already dark, Maronka opened the wooden plank door and took me up to the shed where I could look through the cracks and see icicles dripping from the eaves and woodpeckers hammering at the trees. Sometimes she brought an apple and thick cream! It was March, and Maronka announced that these were the sounds of spring. The sharp clean air, the wonderful smell of hay, made me giddy with happiness. I could peer out of the cracks in the barn and find snowdrops even in the dark. My eyes were so adapted to darkness that they almost acquired the magical gift of the blind. Even in winter I could see small birds' footprints in the snow. Maronka also allowed me to run carefully around the cowshed without disturbing the animals. She became my saint and savior, and I waited impatiently each long, dark day for her to appear.

What was I to do with the solitude and silence? I wanted to sleep and dream of a different kind of day, one that lasted forever, a day that would take hours to fade, where everything was mysterious and remote and beautiful. I imagined soft, balmy, velvety rains, violets springing up in the grass, frogs croaking in the nearby swamp, the sky, tall flowers, and still water, all kept in suspended sepia daylight. I was master of the alchemy of time in my universe.

Sometimes, using a tiny kerosene lamp, Mother read fairytales supplied by Maronka. They inspired even more daydreams. Thousands of images blossomed in my solitude. I imagined medieval maidens with flying hair captured by cannibals, knights wounded in battle, their wounds bathed by damsels in grottos, and saints killing dragons. As she read, I imagined stepping into the pictures and riding my hobbyhorse along a painted path of silent trees. The best daydream was Sleeping Beauty. The cellar was my castle! Instead of a bed made of boards and packed straw, I was asleep on a beautiful puffed bed, in an enchanted castle, where I was waiting for the prince to kiss me awake.

My nightmare was *Little Red Riding Hood* and *Hansel and Gretel*. As I walked into my grandmother's bedroom, the Big Bad Wolf, whose sharp white teeth reminded me of the Gestapo dogs, was waiting to eat me. At the same time little Gretel was about to be shoved into the burning oven by the old witch.

I had always had a wild imagination, even when I was very little. When I closed my eyes I felt happy. The visions and adventures that passed before my closed eyes were an escape into another life. Despite my little bed of straw and boards, I felt free. I dreamed vividly and often, and images of dreams were etched on my mind when I awoke. Many times, I believed that a dream was reality, and the reality a dream. I could stop time and cause anything to happen.

My favorite imagined activity was looking for mushrooms. The search was my main source of delight. Rainy weather would bring out these beautiful fungi under the firs, birches, and aspens. I could feel the dark, damp moss, rich earth, and rotting leaves. I was there with Klara the cook and Olga and we all had big baskets. Sometimes, I reported that

I'd seen dwarfs sleeping underneath the shrubs, and that we should be careful not to make noise and wake them. On overcast afternoons, we set out on our long gathering hunt in the drizzle, and returned before dinnertime, glowing with contentment. We spread out our trophies on a wooden table and gloried in our treasures before the cook bundled them off to the kitchen to fry them in butter thickened with sour cream. How delicious the mushrooms were at the dinner table! We experienced a state of grace.

In winter, when the bunker was very cold and damp, I sat on my "bed," tipped my head backwards, imagined a glimpse of the sky, and willed the brilliance of a sunset to warm my body.

Sometimes, the creaking of Buma and Donia's bed woke me up. Their lovemaking frightened me. I could not imagine the reason for the groans, moans, sighs, and cries. They were in love. Why were they jostling and having a fight? Why were they hurting each other? Eventually the commotion ended, and I was happy they were quiet and liked each other again.

Sleep was my refuge. I was able to escape into my bottomless darkness as days and nights drifted along endlessly. I felt safe in my sleeping space. Maronka's heavy pillow was another bosom. The down quilt protected me from the terror outside, and I spent my time sleeping, daydreaming, or waiting to be allowed into the barn.

Sounds and strange steps from above were much more dangerous and forbidding than the creaking of Buma and Donia's mattress. Many times, German soldiers and Ukrainian policemen ran through Demko's farm looking for escaped Jews or partisans. We heard growling dogs and the sound of boots searching for prey above our heads.

My mother came to my bed and desperately held me, stroking my hand to make sure I remained perfectly calm and quiet. I sat hidden in the darkness, listening and not believing. Not a whimper, not a cry. Somehow fear gave me strength, for I knew that crying meant death.

Terror intruded only once on us. I was lying motionless in bed, busy with my daydreams, when the boards above cracked and suddenly gave way. A brief flash of panic flew from my mother's eyes, and we all became completely still. Very soon, small hooves appeared through the boards, and a frightened little calf fell down with a huge thud. It started kicking and braying beside me on the mattress. I screamed. Instantly, my father was there, shoving a pillow in my face. He was choking me, and I couldn't see or breathe. Why was he hurting me? The calf was not my doing! While he held me, afraid and motionless, others managed to push the calf back up through our ceiling and into the barn, and to cover the hole.

Maronka waited a very long time before she allowed me to play in the barn again. It was also a long time before I could ride my hobby horse, go mushroom or berry picking with Olga, smell the sharp air of the fir forests, wade in the river, or run barefoot and free in the meadows of my mind. Soon I wouldn't be sleeping as much anymore.

13
MISTΔKEN
IDENTITY

MY BROTHER, JANEK, was born in 1939, just months before the German invasion of Poland. The only photograph that remains of him was taken in a photographer's studio in Zloczów when he was a toddler, before he and Babcia disappeared. It shows a pink-faced little boy with delicate features sitting on a small, plush upholstered armchair and holding a big ball in his right hand. He has flaxen straight hair, a pug nose, high cheeks, and big and curious eyes. He is wearing a military suit, white stockings, and sensible children's walking shoes.

With our move to Babcia's house, his routine had been upset, and he cried and fussed a lot. Even chamomile tea didn't help quiet him down. As a noisy toddler, he could not have gone for the ride to Podhorce to our new summerhouse. Babcia had decided that she would take him to a quieter town where her sister lived and they would be safe. After all, England and France were fighting Germany. France had the strongest army in Europe, and the British ruled the seas. Hitler would be destroyed in no time. Even though we had received the news about the fire in the synagogue in Brody, my mother and I never gave up hope of seeing Grandmother Hancia and Janek again.

In the bunker, Mother lay in her bed as if in a trance. She spoke very little, even to me and Donia, and looked at me as if I did not quite belong to her. As if she didn't deserve to have me alive. I think she was afraid that, if she got too close to me, she would lose me as well. That was fine with me, because I questioned my own identity. After all, I was Zosia now, and in my games I was hiding from the bad people and soldiers and policemen who were after us, as well as from myself.

Almost two years after we went into the bunker, the Russians came down the pitted clay road that meandered through destroyed and burned villages. Only jutting chimneys remained standing or leaning.

They came on horse-drawn wagons, gun carriages, and slow, heavy tanks. Their faces were young but tired, their uniforms dirty, their military caps sitting rakishly on their heads. Hand-carved wooden spoons stuck out from the creased tops of their boots. When they stopped, they pulled out the spoons, ate their soup and kasha, wiped the spoons on their pants, and stuck them back into their boots. They advanced for several days and nights. They were chasing the Germans back to Berlin, Father said.

I stared wide-eyed at the tanks, as big as houses, sweeping down the road, at the young smiling soldiers. Their happiness and anticipation reminded me of my excitement on our swimming outings with Olga before the war. They played accordions or harmonicas and drank huge quantities of vodka, denatured alcohol, and cologne—whatever they could get their hands on. I had seen Russian soldiers in Zloczów when the war began, but these boys looked very young, no older than Rysiek, Demko's son, who was sixteen.

"The Russians have already lost all their regulars," my father said.

My mother looked at them sadly. "These are children. They left mothers at home. They can be killed too, and leave mothers crying." She hurriedly wiped away her tears. "You see, we survived! We survived the Germans. The war is just about over. You'll see, everything is going to change."

"Mamusia, why are you whispering?" I was confused. "We should be singing and dancing with the friendly red-cheeked Russian soldiers."

"We still can't talk loudly. For now, no one should know that we are Jews."

But a glimmer of hope appeared on my mother's bewildered face, and her cheeks turned rosy. I understood that she was waiting for a miracle—to find Babcia and Janek alive and well and for all of us to embrace each other. I suppressed my worst fears and hoped with all my heart.

"We must make our way to Zloczów and see who survived," she said. I did not answer. "Why don't you answer me?" she continued. "Don't you even remember Janek and Babcia Hancia and Grandpa Mendel?"

Mother had discovered my secret! She was right. I'd tried so hard to forget, and forgetting about them was a very bad thing for me to do. I wanted to apologize.

The family decided to spend another night in the bunker and leave the farm the next day. I didn't like the idea of another departure and wanted to stay. I liked the animals, and especially the calf, which had grown big and gentle. I also loved the heavy pillow and the down quilt, where I entertained myself with daydreams.

It was beautiful to be outside in the fresh air. The sun sparkled on the whitewashed wooden walls of the farmhouse, and the galvanized roof looked like a mirror. Summer sunlight radiated from every direction. I sat with my back against the house and looked down at myself. My legs did not belong to me. They were thin as lengths of rope knotted at the knees. My tender skin dripped where muscle used to be. The heat pressed down. Pink cosmos, red gladioli, and tall white daisies stood at attention in the garden. The world was full of cheerful noises. The linden trees shimmered, the poplars fluttered, and in the distance crowns of pines rustled in the warm wind. Again, I could run in the gold, red, and blue fields, with cornflowers and poppies blooming among the wheat!

Our hosts tried to convince us to stay longer. "Zloczów is destroyed. The war is not over yet, and there is nothing to eat in town. Where will you go with a child? It is dangerous for Jews to travel. It's summer. You can spend nights anywhere, and soon our hut will be livable again. You can send Zosia for lessons. Who knows how long it will be before they open any schools."

Maronka begged and cajoled, but Demko paid no attention to his wife. He and his brother Stefan were busy preparing a big feast to celebrate the end of the war. In the kitchen, Demko was roasting a small pig that crackled on the fire, giving off the most wonderful smells, while Rysiek peeled huge quantities of potatoes and Maronka chopped cabbage. Stefan was in charge of the samogon, homemade vodka brewed from potatoes and dripped through a rubber pipe into a kettle. These trophies were pulled out of the deep recesses of a secret cellar, and displayed on the table.

As we sat around the feast, Demko and Stefan alternated toasts, which addressed good people of all nationalities, even Jews. There were even apologies for the *nepriyatnosti* (unpleasant events) the Germans and local police had inflicted on the good Jewish people.

"We were afraid to trade the gold pieces for money," Demko said, "because our neighbors could have found out that we were hiding Jews, and someone could have reported on us to the Germans."

After a while, Demko was completely drunk and began telling a story. "Your grandmother Hancia was a real merchant, the best in town. After the Bolsheviks took Mendel away and the Germans came, she knew what to do with your father's money. She deposited many gold pieces with Pan Apolek, the miller, and Pan Apolek paid us once a month.

"He is very Christian, like us, you know, but a very honest man totally devoted to Mendel's business and family.

"Yes, Pani Geller, your mother, Pani Hancia, was a very smart woman. It wasn't just enough to have money, you know. She was a shrewd merchant and knew how to pay. If she didn't know that, it would have cost you your lives. If she'd paid us in advance, we would have gotten rid of you sooner. The Germans were here too long. They marched through the property with their dogs and the Ukrainian police, sniffing out Jews. You were lucky that the neighbors didn't inform. Envious neighbors can be mean when someone makes money by hiding Jews. They spied on their own kin and informed. Five kilograms of sugar for each Jew."

Stefan began playing his harmonica, and Demko slapped his knees in rhythm.

"You know, my friends, the war was too long. At first, we thought, what the hell, Mendel's family are nice people, and Mendel gave me lots of credit when times were hard, and I can sure use the money to fix the house and the barn. But then there was no end to this *koshmar* (nightmare). Shootings in Jelechowice, pogroms, murders. Gestapo and Ukrainian police all over the place looking for Jews, informers. And then the last straw, the nail in the coffin—an edict that we would be killed for hiding Jews. It was too much. I started drinking in the morning. I couldn't sleep at night. Maronka had attacks of nerves and cried."

He stood up and raised his hands. "I will hack them to death with my ax, I decided. Stefan will help me. One at a time. My dear Pani Geller," he reached out and kissed my mother's hand.

"You were the biggest problem, my dear Pani Geller. Two years in the cellar, too many potatoes, too much bread. You are plump and beautiful. Just like a wealthy farmer's wife. Pan Buma and Pan Geller would be easy. They are men like us. We were going to save Donia for last, and make love to her first. You are so beautiful, Donia. Your eyes, your soft breasts. You make me so happy, you make my cock stand up."

I listened. I knew she was beautiful but I couldn't understand the words about the cock. Chickens live in the chicken house and lay warm eggs. Roosters live there, too. What is the connection between chickens and roosters and Donia's being beautiful? And Demko didn't mention me at all! I didn't count, and I was not important to anyone. Or maybe they did not plan on killing me. Anger, spite, but worst of all, terror overcame me. But this time it seemed like a story with singing, dancing, and delicious food. It was crazy. I wanted to run away right there and then. I will miss Maronka and the barn animals, and especially the calf, I thought. Also the big puffy pillow and down quilt where I spent endless time.

The next evening, we rushed to say farewell to our Ukrainian hosts and made our way by wagon with other travelers to Zloczów. Everyone was silent. There was no laughter, no rejoicing. What kind of victory was this?

In the wagon, my mother told no one that we were Jews. She only said that it had been a long time since she had heard any news about her mother and younger son, and that perhaps her father was in Siberia. Only on the last part of the journey, when a Russian truck was taking us to Zloczów, did she say she was a Jew returning to the town where she'd been born and grown up, and where her family lived. She said that she feared that something bad had happened to them. After all, so many bad things had happened in two years. She sobbed when she talked about it, and strangers tried to comfort her as best as they could. "Don't worry, don't worry, it can't be so bad. The Germans didn't kill all the Jews."

An older man on the truck joined the conversation. "Good thing that Hitler annihilated so many of them before the Russians returned. The ones who are left are joining the Russians to kill the rest of us." We were all silent for the rest of the trip as the truck drove along furrows plowed by tanks.

Zloczów no longer existed. It had been blown up by guns, burned down, trampled upon by boots. The wind blew over the streets and pavements of my childhood. Our little town had died abruptly in the war, as if mowed down by a big sharp scythe. People were pulling broken furniture out of the ashes of gutted buildings: tabletops, armoires, metal locks, iron tools. The lucky ones found their hidden jewelry. We walked from one fire-gutted ruin to another. My mother wanted to run and see the people she had known in Zloczów, to learn everything they knew, but she lost courage and stayed with me, while Buma, Donia, and my father looked for information. We stood at the center of the marketplace, among the ruins.

From the square, you could see all of Zloczów. The church steeple pierced the clouds, and through the gaps of rubble and burned-out houses, the open meadows, the sheaves of hay in the fields, the forest, and the road to the train station looked the same. Grandfather Mendel's warehouse had been burned to the ground, and the synagogue had been destroyed. Our grief was so intense that it made us feel as if centuries had passed. People looked at us as if we had returned from the hereafter, and marveled, "Can it be you're alive?"

We didn't like that question. Some stared; some kept examining us, trying to get a better look. They were surprised that we were still alive. At some point even we ourselves began to feel surprise, as if we had lived too long.

In town refugees were gathering in the old school house. Everyone still had fear in their eyes. Some were returning from concentration camps and forests, some from Russia. The schoolhouse had a kitchen, and the Russian soldiers unloaded sacks of potatoes and corn, kegs of honey, and crates of apples and vegetables for the refugees.

When we got to the schoolhouse, Mamusia declared that Stefan was surely mistaken. Babcia and Janek must have escaped. After all, he hadn't seen the fire, and he hadn't seen them in that synagogue either. Perhaps they had returned and were looking for us in town. "We must find your brother and grandma, and surely Grandpa Mendel will be coming back from Russia. The rails have been repaired, and some trains from the east are running."

As I watched my mother's red cheeks and glittering eyes, I could almost see images of her son and parents in her mind.

She was speaking to me, but I didn't answer. Her words had made my skin crawl. At that precise moment, I was not sure any more that my brother was alive. I couldn't hear his laughing or crying any more, or feel his little hands pulling at my hair or ears. Suddenly, he was silent, and I had no choice but to imagine his face. Even in daylight, in the cold drizzle, I recognized his smile, and I was confused, no longer certain of anything.

Father, Donia, and Buma were tired and despondent. Donia's eyes were red, her face smudged by tears. In town they'd heard about those who had been killed or burned, who had been shipped to Belz, Bergen Belsen, Janowska, or who had been lucky to escape to the forests, find poison, or squeeze and jump through the narrow cattle car windows. Mother just listened, relieved that there was no specific news of Babcia and Janek. Suddenly, she began speaking. "You know Frydzia, the baker's daughter? She survived in the forest, and she's here in the schoolhouse. She tells me that there are still people hiding in the forest who don't know about the Russian victory. Tomorrow, she will take me with her to search the places she knows."

Mother and Frydzia set off early in the morning on their mission. The August sun shone jaggedly through the trees.

Suddenly, they approached an encampment with a few men and what looked like a family. A young, disheveled woman with wild eyes was nursing her child. Another, a four-year-old, was running around, followed by an older woman pleading with him to stop. Several bearded, unkempt men with wild and frightened eyes were guarding the encampment with knives and one rifle.

"*Amcha! Amcha!*" (Your people!) Frydzia shouted to the group. "The war is over! The Germans ran away! The Russians have liberated us. They have food and housing for us. You don't have to hide anymore. You can go back to town. We only came here hoping to find some lost relatives."

They looked at her in awe and disbelief. The man holding the rifle put it down and waved them into the camp. Mother had seen the young boy from afar, but coming closer, a terrible excitement gripped her as she looked into the child's eyes. The eyes, the sparkle, the shape of the lips, seemed familiar. She trembled, and her heart fluttered, though when the child came closer, it was not Janek.

Frydzia and Mother helped the group gather their belongings —a very dirty down quilt, some pots and pans, an old suitcase filled with a man's woolen suit, a frayed sheepskin jacket, mittens and wool caps sour with the smell of dampness and mildew. They led them down the road to the schoolhouse. Frydzia carried the young boy, while Mother guided the older woman by her arm.

"You remember me," the woman said. "I am Rifka, the printer's wife. I remember you, Yetka, you are Hancia and Mendel's daughter. You look just like my Frumka, my oldest, who was shot by the *Banderowce*. The little boy survived and is her child, my grandson."

The group returned to town, exhausted, spent, and hungry, but Mother's pain was unrelieved. She remembered and cried, and hoped with all her heart. For her, my brother and Babcia still existed. Maybe it didn't happen after all, I thought. Maybe it's only a story. Stefan didn't see it happen, he was only told about the fire. Perhaps he mistook someone else's child for Janek and Babcia. I resolved that, when I grew up, we would search the world far and wide for them. Maybe they had emigrated to one of those strange places, like Shanghai or Venezuela or New York. We were strong, and our longing would help us find them.

14
THE WEDDING

A MONTH AFTER LIBERATION, in
August 1944, Donia and Buma decided to start life over again
and get married in Zlozców.

A Jewish wedding usually cannot be a happy event.
Nobody has as many dead to lament, and certainly no one
had as many as they did that August.

For the ceremony, a *tallis* was used for the *chupa*, and the
printer's wife gave Donia a beautiful new silk-embroidered
scarf to cover her head. The bride had no family at all, so my
father's friend, Dr. Salo, who survived the war fighting in
Russia, and his wife Sonia, accompanied her to the canopy.
My parents walked arm in arm with Buma. Then the groom

recited the Kaddish for his departed parents and all his nearest of kin, except for his beloved brother Pipa. He could still be alive. He could return, and it would have been sacrilege to mourn the living.

The last time he had seen Pipa was when he bartered my father's watch for a handgun and left for the forest to join the Soviet partisans. When the victorious and bedraggled Russian army liberated our area, Buma and Donia had relentlessly searched for news, but with no success. The partisans had not heard of any Pipa or Pinchas-Schloyme in the forests, and the Russian soldiers were too happy and too drunk to perform due diligence for a young Jewish university student who had once joined the partisans and was probably dead.

Forty survivors out of a town of thirty thousand gathered at the wedding. Some partisans and a group of "foreign comrades," Hassidim from Chelm, also showed up. We didn't know how the Hassidim had survived or reached Zloczów. Their eyes were fixed on God and they ignored the commotion. The eyes of other guests were mostly fixed on the ground because a glance into someone's eye, one word, one gesture, one name carelessly spoken, was enough to spoil the mood.

The wedding took place in the schoolhouse. The big

room was lit by electric bulbs that the Russians connected with long, thick cables to batteries in the courtyard. Tables were arranged in a horseshoe shape, with two pictures, both cut from posters, nailed to the wall—one of Marshal Stalin, the other of a woman standing at a loom from which rays surged in all directions.

Maronka and Rysiek came from the farm to help my mother with the party and prepared sausage and pickles and beef stew. Russian soldiers and officers also came. Many were already tipsy and laughing. Some brought their cameras to record what was for them the first Jewish wedding after the liberation. They were going to give the pictures to a war correspondent covering the Western front. Men and women in uniform and a colonel also came to the wedding. They brought lots of vodka, and two soldiers brought their accordions, too. The Russians were determined to make the atmosphere friendly and cordial. "Let's drink to our motherland! Let's drink to Stalin!" They urged everybody to eat and drink with them, and would be offended if anyone refused. So no one refused, not even the Hassidim from Chelm.

Since no rabbi was to be found, Mr. Goldberg, a learned and religious man dressed in a dark pre-war suit, officiated and wrote the *ketubah*. He was a friend of Donia's father and had survived by hiding under his own bakery. His hands were clasped as if in prayer. "A town perished," he called out. "You can imagine grief if only one family, or every other family, perishes, and the others are still alive. Then you can grieve. Or if one person from every family in town survived, and if all the survivors stood in the marketplace and wept together. But it's not that way! It's not the usual kind of human tragedy. It's beyond human measure. We who are here cannot really feel or understand what happened. This is how nature protects us."

"*Mazal tov!* Drink, Buma. After all, it's your wedding!"

"I never imagined my wedding would be like this," Buma said to my mother. He poured himself a glass of vodka. He poured one for her, too. "Believe me, never like this," he said, draining the glass. "My brother and sister, my parents, should be here." He was drinking a lot.

"What's the difference?" another guest said. "The most important thing is that you are having a wedding at all, Buma. That you are still alive. That we are alive!"

A soldier began playing. He alternated between lively and wistful songs on his accordion, while other soldiers sang along, their voices dolefully hushed, or jumped up, slapped their thighs and boots, and raced across the floor in a frantic

Cossack dance. Donia had sewn a dress for me from some old material a woman gave her. It was blue, patterned with deeper blue cornflowers. It was festive and beautiful. I felt very special and important. Now that I was Szaneczka again, a glint in my eyes, and a faint smile, instinctively emerged on my face. I was dancing around with two other Jewish children, happy that the Russians had enlivened the sad party.

When the soldiers grew tired, they asked for Jewish songs and dances. Zhenia, who was the most musical and knew all the Jewish songs, stood up, swallowed some vodka, and walked to the middle of the room. She put two fingers in her mouth and whistled so shrilly that the children jumped. Bent at the waist, she danced, looking at her feet, flinging her head and arms about, and snapping her fingers. The children and soldiers picked up the beat but, since we had trouble snapping our fingers, we clapped our hands. Zhenia called out to the Russians to dance with her. The Russians swallowed more vodka and jumped into the middle of the floor. Green shirts shining, revolvers strapped to their waist, they laughingly began to imitate Hassidic gestures of religious rapture. My mother and Donia lowered their heads, their arms fell to their sides, and their bodies shook with sobs. Zhenia looked around, understood the sadness, covered her mouth with her hand, and also burst into tears.

A military commissar began exhorting the bewildered Jews. "Glory to the motherland! You are the power. Everything here belongs to you. There are no more masters!"

A Russian lieutenant proposed a toast. "To the married couple! *Gorko, gorko, gorko!*" The Russians toasted everyone and everything without end. Still another soldier called me over, stood me on the table, and ordered, "Let's drink to our motherland, to Stalin!" He told me to recite after him in Russian. I had no idea what he was saying but felt it was terribly important that I get it right:

"I am a little flower, I am a young pioneer. I am Stalin's little daughter, defender of the USSR."

The Russians clapped and laughed. A woman soldier gave me a red scarf and told me I was now a Pioneer, defending the motherland.

"What good is it? I lost one child, my family," my mother whispered.

"Stop it, Yetka," someone interrupted. "This is a wedding. This is a wedding party! What's wrong with you? Is this what you survived for? To sit around and feel bad for the rest of your life?"

"How can we forget? That's something we can't ever forget," another woman said. "Besides, the *goyim* will always remind us that we are Jews and have mongrel children. All the blood and terrible memories: where can we run from that?"

"Get those looks off your faces, people!" A Jewish partisan with a sunny disposition had raised his glass. "Backward, ignorant Jews. You don't have to be afraid anymore! Communism will give you true equality. Jews are even favored now!"

Everyone, including the Hassidim, perked up. "Stalin is the Red Messiah," one said. "We'll strangle Hitler's gang. We'll hang Goebbels and Goehring! Hurrah!"

"To a new life! *L'Chaim!*" they shouted as a soldier began playing a lively, rhythmic Russian song on his accordion. Zhenia and we children joined the Russians in the singing and dancing. Mr. Goldberg and my father recited old Jewish prayers in Hebrew: "Thanks unto Thee, O Lord our God, that Thou hast let us live and witness this day." A Hassid's voice rang out as he broke the bread with his monastic fingers. "Blessed is the God of Israel, who has chosen us among all the peoples of the world." He blessed the food, and we sat down at the table. Buma's hand was on Donia's thigh. "It's alright now, Donia. We are man and wife."

More Jewish prayers ended the wedding party, and the guests, including the Hassidim, were soon preparing to leave. Since there was no vodka left, Rysiek began piling up chairs and sweeping cigarette butts from the floor, while Maronka gathered blackened frying pans and misshapen enamel saucepans and platters into a large duffel bag. Mother and Father, Buma and Donia, were also silent as they sat against the wall with the pictures of Stalin and the lady with many sunrays in the background.

Suddenly, two strangers burst into the room. It was Pipa and a woman!

Buma and Pipa stood opposite each other in disbelief. They ran to each other, kissed each other on the lips, and shook hands with such force that it looked as if they were trying to tear each other's arms off. Distraught, still throwing their arms around each other's necks, they continued kissing tenderly like drunks.

"Fate hunted me down and brought me here, Buma! Destiny told me to look for you in this place!"

He was the same Pipa I remembered, but he was also very different. He was now a lieutenant in the Soviet army and a happy man. He was more filled out. His gait was decisive. He had a disheveled mop of blond hair, a ruddier complexion, and strong muscles, but the same laughing eyes and big, warm hands. A green uniform with many medals, well-polished German boots, a revolver on his belt, and several gold Swiss watches on his hand completed the picture. He lifted me, smothered my face with kisses, and swung me around like an airplane.

"The war is over!" he shouted. "We have food to eat, and all the roads are open. It's hard to understand, but it's over! Tomorrow, day will break, and I won't have to attack, shoot anymore, or hide."

"Why didn't you come with us to the bunker? Where were you? How did you survive?" my father asked in disbelief.

Pipa snorted and sighed and sank into a chair. "I am not ashamed of not being dead. Being alive isn't a crime. I was determined to live in the open air and get *nekomeh*—you know, revenge," he said to me, "by killing Germans. I heard partisans were fighting near Bryansk. That was a three days' walk. The railroad was thirty kilometers away, the woods very thick, the roads full of mud. I was lost. During the night, heavy and low clouds covered the sky, but at four in the morning, in the rain, I sensed a special creaking and rustling, unlike the storm or the movement of animals. A group of Jewish partisans found me." He jumped up. "They were on the run. They'd been driven away from their old camp and stumbled upon me. They were going through a bad time, without food, in dangerous territory, in search of a new campsite. And there, in the mysterious silence of the forest, I finally found my calling. The commander accepted me without question. They had only two guns. They had been attacked by a Ukrainian group that took away their weapons. So my handgun came in handy. The Ukrainians were the most dangerous in those woods. The Germans organized, armed, and indoctrinated them, as if there was any need for that! Poles and Jews are their natural enemies. The commander remarked, 'Welcome to the Partisan Republic of the Marshes! You can hunt the hunters with us!'

"Soon, the Soviets parachuted men to join the bands of partisans into one fighting force, and we began building a new camp. We had two log huts half buried in the ground, camouflaged with turf and branches to make them invisible from the air. The forest and swamps made the rest of the camp accessible only to Russian planes that dropped weapons and supplies, especially sacks of flour and salt, which we traded with villagers for chickens, eggs, lard, and honey.

"We were in constant contact with Moscow, receiving

news and instructions from the 'Great Land,' the Soviet territory beyond the front. The field radio was our most valuable possession, and the partisan who manned it was both saint and surgical technician," Pipa explained in quiet detail, as if planning another attack in that schoolhouse. "Sometimes I imagined I was hunting for dangerous animals with my father in the forests of Volhynia. One day I heard that our house in Wlodzimierz had been burned, that only Bella had jumped from a window and been immediately shot.

"My hunting skills, my fury, and a thirst for revenge for our murdered family made me a valued fighter. I was consumed with rage and the sport of hunting the hunters. I felt calmer and more peaceful whenever I shot a German or a Ukrainian.

"One day an order came to blow up a railway line used for transporting German ammunition, wounded soldiers, and supplies, and I was the first to volunteer. I set out with a group of ten men, but since the target was a long distance from our camp we had to move across open terrain in daylight. Bullets flew, as our men came under machine gun fire. We managed to blow up the railroad line, but four men did not return. I was carried back to camp with a German bullet in my foot." He pulled off his boot to show us his mangled right leg.

"When the radio brought news of the German retreat

from Stalingrad, Red Army soldiers appeared in the camp almost immediately. We were ecstatic. The Russian soldiers sang, danced, and kissed each other. Two days after liberation, we moved to a German command post. The Russians let us do whatever we wanted. Our boys brought in many escaping Germans. I felt a warm but bitter taste when I shot a German prisoner for the first time. One time one of them refused to clean a latrine, and I ordered one of our boys to make him clean it, and then drown him in it, on the spot. Another time our boys brought some Germans in a wagon. We poured gasoline over them and the wagon and burned them. The wagon was burning day and night for two days. Did I have feelings? I had feelings for the horses. We saved the horses. It was not the horses' fault. But the Germans had burned us and our children."

Pipa rose from his chair and began pacing the room. He stretched his big hands upward, as if begging for mercy. His cheeks glistened with sweat, his smooth forehead was tense. His blue eyes darkened and narrowed, almost closed with pain, and his broad mouth was pursed shut.

"Do you want something to eat, something to drink?" Mother asked, gently touching his shoulder. She wanted him to stop. But he didn't.

Instead, he dove into a chair and pointed his finger at Buma, becoming more and more outraged as he obsessively pushed on with his tale. "Soon after our victory, I was walking with a buddy in Bryansk and spotted a Ukrainian behind us cursing the Soviets and the Jews. When we passed a house with a courtyard, I glanced around, grabbed the man, took him into the courtyard and finished him off. 'One anti-Semite less,' I said as I returned my knife into my jacket. We lost six million. Six million is enough."

In the spring of 1944, Pipa's group commandeered a Russian freight truck and joined the Russian advance west, all the way to Berlin. After the fall of Berlin, he found Rita, now his fiancée. They met and fell in love in Germany, on the way to Potsdam, and made love in the Reichstag.

It was past midnight when Pipa finished his story. The woman who had come with him had been sitting silently for hours. She was a blond, broad-faced, red faced, plump, and smiling Russian woman in a very tight soldier's uniform. Under it, she was wearing a silk blouse with black polka dots, and was happily pregnant. Pipa ventured an embarrassed smile when he finally introduced Comrade Rita to us. "Now we will celebrate two Russian weddings!" he shouted as Rita began unpacking their own sausages and vodka, chocolates, and a can of American pineapple juice for me. From his pocket, Pipa also pulled out a large can of caviar and bread. The bride laughed and sang beautifully, while our soldier cousin accompanied her on the harmonica. They were enchanted with life and each other. Pipa said they were leaving for Kiev the next day to visit her family and have a proper Soviet ceremony in the Palace of Weddings.

"*L'Chaim* to our new life," he said as he poured vodka for the grown-ups and pineapple juice for me. No religion could dispute their good fortune. "We are going to look for a place in the world where our baby can be born in peace, and that place is our motherland."

Rita was still laughing when they left the schoolhouse. Just as he had been determined to fight the enemy, he was now determined to make a new life for himself and his new family as a decorated Jewish officer in the New Russia. Bewildered, we all waved good-bye. Rita continued to laugh and throw kisses to us.

That night was far from a wedding night of bliss.

Donia and Buma, drowsy, eyes half closed, lay together on an army cot they found. Mother and Father were dozing. I curled up on my mother's lap and bosom and dreamed of finding and hugging Janek. Or of already having found him, and he was here, curled up and sleeping with me. I couldn't tell for sure.

From the balconies in Zloczów, red flags flapped. They still bore the shadow of the black swastikas that had been unstitched. On Tuesday, August 7, 1945, came news of the atomic bomb dropped on Hiroshima, on the same day Mother, Father, Buma, Dina, and I smuggled ourselves out of Poland and into Czechoslovakia, and from there to a displaced persons' camp in Germany.

15
WHITE LINEN AND WHITE BREAD

WHEN WE REACHED the displaced persons' camp in Germany, our family was given a separate small "apartment" in barracks that had formerly housed the German Air Force, the Luftwaffe. We were unusual among survivors because we were a family—not intact, but still a mother, father, and child. We were in Deggendorf, in the American Zone, where the American soldiers didn't know what to do first for the thin, pale, and frightened people in our barracks.

Europe was still in turmoil: spouses looking for each other, parents seeking children, children trying to remember who their real parents were. People were waiting for days at railway stations, waving photographs at those arriving from camps. Cries of "Have you seen my husband? My child? My mother? My father?" echoed throughout Europe's bombed-out rail yards. Refugees packed the Displaced Persons' camp. There were Hungarians and Russians in better shape than the Polish Jews who had returned from concentration camps; Jewish men who had defected from the Polish-Russian army; families from the Soviet Union. Many survivors from other cities and towns in Poland, like us, showed up daily.

Our apartment was luxurious compared to Demko's dugout. The beds were wide, the sheets white, the mattresses springy. A night table with a reading lamp stood beside each bed, and a small iron stove, with lots of stacked wood, provided heat.

We had green blankets with US stamped on them, pillows, and pots, pans, and cooking utensils for our portable benzene stoves. They were all of first-class quality. My father always said that the Germans knew how to make the best of everything. Mother made sure she collected all the necessary extra cooking utensils—a meat grinder, a wooden mixing bowl, and a sieve, a *drushlak,* for noodles.

The JOINT Distribution Committee helped people like us. They issued a small, untuned upright piano for lessons that my mother had requested for me. I also got an excellent two-wheel German bicycle and a German sled from a warehouse where there were also lots of German skis and small boxes of postage stamps with Hitler's face on them. When the American soldiers accompanied us to the warehouse, they'd grab a handful of stamps and throw them up in the air like confetti. They encouraged me to do the same, but I was still afraid.

The U.S. Army commissary distributed all the basic staples, including cigarettes, raisins, and thick chocolate bars, tea, coffee, and canned peaches (an exotic fruit we had never tasted), American condensed milk, American ground sardines, American powdered eggs. We brushed our teeth with American toothbrushes, swallowed American vitamins, and my father took to chain-smoking American Camels. Besides canned peaches, chewing gum was also new to me. I got plenty of it from the American soldiers who chewed gum a lot and showed us how. "You have to chew, but never swallow or you'll choke," one explained. "It tastes like peppermint leaves. After a while it stops tasting, but you can keep it in your mouth until nighttime. Then you stick it someplace until morning, so you can chew it some more."

"I chew it like the Americans do," I boasted to my friends

as I bit down hard for a few seconds and created a wonderful little crackling pop. I was proud of this new American peppermint experience. I knew about food that I had to chew before swallowing, but this was something new. I put all five pieces of gum in my mouth at once and chewed and chewed the big ball of greenish-gray stuff, then saved it for the next day to chew again.

The refugee camp also contained a common room with an American ping pong table and card tables. Near the common room was a dispensary, or what we called "the sanitarium," a veranda with wooden deck chairs and bright artificial lamps with which the children were irradiated. I was allowed to lounge on a deck chair and listen to American music on the radio. "You Are My Sunshine, My Only Sunshine," was my favorite song.

Many other activities took place in the common room. We saw concerts and pre-war Jewish films, such as The Dybbuk and The Town of Belz. Too many people wanted to get in, so the place was packed. People squeezed and pushed. Suddenly lights went out and complete silence reigned. When the well-known song came on—"Oh Belz, my beloved Belz, my *shtetele* Belz where all my family. . . ."—terrible cries burst out everywhere, a collective groan of pain. People covered their eyes and faces with their hands and stood up to get a better look. I couldn't hear the melody or the words of the song, and I couldn't see the screen. This went on until the film ended.

Besides films and concerts, many weddings were celebrated in the common room. Gambling, and heated political discussions, also took place there. People were very afraid. They needed to buy dollars, and dollars were expensive. Money was needed for travel expenses and life in those distant foreign lands where no one knew us and perhaps didn't want to. The most popular activity was playing cards, and the most popular game was poker. The games were serious and purposeful, their aim personal victory, not relaxation or socializing. Congeniality began and ended with reporting the name of the *lager*, the concentration camp players had come from. Everyone tried to win and save as much money as possible. Others also did business by speculating. They bought merchandise, sold it quickly at a profit, and bought more dollars.

Army caps, hats of political parties, and various kinds of epaulets were especially popular. Big Polish army caps that fell over the eyes and ears, six-pointed stars (the insignias of Zionist youth organizations), Russian army caps with red stars, caps with lacquered visors, British Union Jacks, and American Stars and Stripes depicted identification and political allegiance. Younger men scooped up any medals they could find in looted houses and shops and sewed them on their jackets—gold and silver stars with purple and Prussian blue, red and white stripes with crimson ribbons. It was an international kaleidoscope of military adornments!

Political discussions and heated arguments about who'd really won the war were far more exciting to me than cards.

"If it hadn't been for America, it would have been all over for Russia. America sent Russia ammunition, canned goods, warm clothes and boots, everything they needed. What would Russia have done without all that?"

"And what would Americans have done with all their boots and canned food if it hadn't been for the Russians? Would they have done the fighting? The Russians were the best and the bravest."

"That's right, they drink pure alcohol and go on the attack, not afraid of anything!"

"There were twice as many Russians killed as Germans."

"That's because sometimes they were too drunk."

"No, it's because the secret police was right behind them, and they shot any soldier that moved too slow."

"Not true. The NKVD didn't force them. The Russian soldiers threw themselves, with grenades, under German tanks and hurled themselves onto machine guns. Russian pilots didn't jump out of burning planes, but crashed them into the Germans to kill more of them. They were fighting for their motherland."

"I'll tell you why the Russians didn't jump from their burning planes. The NKVD executed anyone who lost a plane. The Americans told their soldiers, 'Don't worry about the airplane, just save yourself and come back.' But to the Russians an ordinary rifle is more important than a man. Russia has the most people in the world. The Russians sent thousands of soldiers to their deaths until the Germans were out of ammunition."

"It's no trick to win when you've got so many tanks and airplanes."

A Zionist jumped on the table, shouting, "You're all idiots! If Germany hadn't attacked Russia first, Russia would have just watched the Germans kill Jews and anybody else they wanted to murder! We have been massacred from the time of the First Temple. The Crusades, the Inquisition, the Worms massacre, the Cossack uprisings. You have to defend yourselves. You all belong in Palestine!"

Since these heated quarrels went nowhere, someone eventually started punching his opponent. Angry fistfights between radical believers broke out. Men were no longer helpless. They could release their anger and bitterness. Since I did not understand the politics, I loved watching these fights. They were like make-believe, because no one was really hurt, and laughter and hugs followed the melee.

Survivors also tried to regain a sense of life by living with and marrying each other. People were trying to help each other by joining together, starting families. The Displaced Persons' camps in Germany marked a new beginning for Jewish life. Jews in Germany were marrying each other quickly and Jewish children were being born. Widowers married widows; invalids married invalids. The blind married the lame, and paralytics the tubercular. An older hunchbacked man in our barracks married a pretty young woman just returned from Auschwitz who could have been his daughter. Everyone was in a hurry, afraid that there wouldn't be enough partners to go around. No one wanted to be left alone.

Every marriageable man was worth his weight in gold, and women weren't being choosy. Their best years were already long past. Their children had been taken from them, and they weren't sure that God, who hadn't been around for a long time, would bless them with others.

Jewish women had to compete with neatly dressed, well-mannered German women who had been lonely for a long time. They were especially nice to younger Jewish men who had come back from Russia and didn't know what the Germans had done to Jews. They offered them clothes that had belonged to their husbands, fathers, and brothers, cleaned their boots, and washed their feet, just so they wouldn't go away.

A blond German woman with a Lorelei-like air about her gave Buma a great black leather jacket, desperately rolling her sad blue eyes and begging him to stay with her. He was bewitched by her charms, and for a moment saw the possibility of another life. As she invited him for supper, his fantasy gave way to anger, and he ran out without saying good-bye or thank you.

"I couldn't marry a German woman," he said decisively when he saw my mother again. She had no idea where he had been or what thoughts were going though him.

"What are you talking about, Buma?" she said. "You're already married, and you'll have a child soon."

Some American soldiers at the Displaced Persons' camp

were Jewish, and some tried to speak Yiddish to me, which I didn't understand. I was also startled when I saw a black man in an American army uniform. It was the first time I had seen a real-life black person. I thought he'd come from the Russian film we saw in Poland, *Belaya obezyana*, or "White Monkey," a very popular Tarzan movie. Its cast included many blacks, so-called "monkey people." Of course I had no idea that this word insulted black people. How, I wondered, had this live "monkey" gotten to Germany? I'd left him in the movie theater in Zloczów a long time ago! His hair was tightly curled and rough, and I wondered how he was able to comb it. His face and arms were brown, the color of milk chocolate, but I was comforted by his white palms. His jolly face and his big, white, shiny teeth fascinated me. Both seemed much larger than the faces and teeth I knew. His forehead was wide and smooth, the nose wide and flat, and I loved his big, sparkling eyes that looked as if they were about to pop out. I also liked his gentle, thick lips and sunny disposition. In short, I was not afraid.

His name was Bill. He was lonely and wanted to make me his friend. I repeated his name, and he asked mine. I was no longer Zosia. I'd gone back to my pre-war name, "Desert Rose," or Shoshana, or Szanka, which Bill found impossible to learn or to pronounce. "You're going to America soon. You need an American name now. Your name is S-U-S-A-N. Repeat after me: 'Hi, my name is Susan. I am going to America.'" He also gave me an American notebook with rustling white pages to write down words and practice my English. I was a little scared of "Hi." That word reminded me of the Gestapo and their "*Heil Hitler*" salutes, so Bill taught me to say "Hello" instead.

What was happening to me? Now that I was Szanka again, I was going to be "Susan." I wasn't even sure I could be the same child I used to be. Who was that child? My entire past was like the hide-and-seek we'd played before the war. With Bill's help, I miraculously had an American name, a new life. "Hello, my name is Susan, and I am going to America soon."

I repeated that sentence again and again. He also supplied my father with extra cigarettes and the children with special pink gum, the kind that made bubbles, which was my favorite. It took a lot of practice to make crackling sounds, and even more to blow rubbery pink bubbles and become a real American. Bill told me that chewing gum grew on rubber trees in America, and I couldn't wait to get to Deh-Lan-Sey Street, so I could see round bubbly pink trees for myself.

After Zloczów, Deggendorf seemed fabulously rich. People would go into houses, through bureaus and wardrobes, and take what they wanted. They brought back kitchen utensils, tableware, bedclothes, bedspreads, towels. If help was needed, they'd ask a soldier to accompany them and, if necessary, force open the door with his rifle butt. Soldiers would say, "Take whatever you want! Take it without asking. It's not their stuff anyway! It's all been stolen."

Once I accompanied Buma and his friends to Munich. My mother couldn't go on these expeditions, because taking other people's things made her sad. The apartment Buma and I visited was nicer than any I had ever seen before. The rooms were furnished in different colors and had shiny parquet floors. Chandeliers dripped with crystals shaped like petals, and icicles hung from ceilings. The walls were decorated with a frieze of pictures of chubby girls with angelic blue eyes and ruddy little boys in Lederhosen, snappy, colorful little green jackets, and caps with feathers. There was a dressing table with a large mirror and its own soft upholstered stool. On the sideboard stood porcelain figures of colorful gnomes sitting on mushrooms, and a pair of lovers kissing at a porcelain well. There were also figurines of women in puffy crinolines, porcelain shepherds fingering piccolos, and plates with chubby pink faces painted on them. I took a little porcelain statue of the gnome in the woods because it reminded me of mushroom hunting before the war. Buma and his friends mostly brought back things from the attics and basements—compasses, whistles, Finnish knives, gas masks, army knapsacks, motorcycle goggles, bayonets, and postage stamp albums.

The more people came to the Displaced Persons' camp, the easier it became to start life over. For Mother, that meant cooking the meals she prepared before the war. The commissary sold meat, sausages, and salamis, and although the products were *treif,* she paid no attention. "At least," she remarked "we don't have to be grateful anymore for Maronka's scraps of bacon and cold potatoes cooked in their skins. Remember, we came from such hunger. We must have great respect for food."

When she had all the products and the kitchen equipment was in place, she made her first big Friday night dinner: chopped liver with onions, soup with real egg noodles, a hen's neck stuffed with flour and chicken fat, carrot *tsimmes,* dumplings soft as pillows put twice through the grinder, and a compote made from apples and plums and American canned peaches. I found it hard to sit at a table properly and eat with a knife and fork, as I was used to eating only with a spoon or with my fingers. I was a wild child learning manners.

"Could I ever have dreamed of eating at a table like this again?" my father asked, thinking of the bunker. "Thanks unto Thee, O Lord our God, that Thou has let us live and witness this day."

That was not all. For Sunday breakfast mother served herring in oil, cottage cheese with radishes, eggs fried with onions, and cakes made with apple and cheese. She was determined to fatten me up before we got to America. Between breakfast and lunch, and lunch and dinner, and at any other time, she would produce slices of sweet, crusty, delicious white bread and butter. She could not stuff enough into my stomach and always carried little emergency parcels wrapped in brown paper in her purse. For snacks after lunch and dinner, I ate yellow noodles with puddles of warm milk and honey. Each week, she put me on the scale in the dispensary to see whether I had gained at least half a kilo to be ready for the trip to America.

To everyone's surprise Donia gave birth to a little girl in Deggendorf. We were all delighted, but there were tears whenever Jews assembled: the more Jews, the more tears.

Also, since the child was a girl, there was no problem with circumcision, to which many were absolutely opposed. So many children had perished because they had been circumcised. My mother startled the group when she declared categorically, "If I had another boy, he would be circumcised. My child would not be afraid of being a Jew."

Buma, Donia, and their child left the displaced persons' camp for America in the summer of 1946. Donia's uncle from Pittsburgh found them through HIAS, the Hebrew Immigrant Aid Society, and made a special trip to Germany to arrange for their affidavits. Louis Ganz, her father's brother, had lots of political clout in Pittsburgh and was one of the owners of the city's largest department store, Horn's. He hired Buma and paid him ten dollars a week, while Donia joined the household staff in their mansion.

Aside from buying food and preparing meals, Mother was buying everything for our trip to America—new pillowcases, shirts, sheets, pajamas. An uncle of hers discovered our name on a list of survivors, and HIAS was supposed to issue papers for the United States any day. She was ecstatic. We were not going to the deserts of Palestine but to relatives who emigrated to escape poverty and anti-Semitism and made a journey to a rich life on Deh-Lan-Cey Street in New York!

Meanwhile, Mother arranged for piano lessons with Frau Doktor Knopf, who came to our apartment twice weekly. She was a tall, lean woman with rolling eyes that protruded from her sockets, and I was a wild and frenzied child, lacked all discipline, couldn't sit still for the scales and repetitions, and hated the whole process. Frau Doktor barked at me in German. I was a little frightened of her because the language reminded me of the Gestapo and their dogs. She showed her expertise and talent by playing the "Moonlight Sonata," a piece I was supposed to learn for the recital. While she swaggered with passion, my mother would wring a dishtowel in her hands and hope that I would start playing soon. But I hated Frau Doktor and the piano lessons. I was never able to count musical time. I only counted time on the clock until I could escape.

Wild and bewildered, I had become a freedom child, and the bike was my passport to open spaces, my instrument of liberty. When we left the dugout, I'd had trouble seeing and walking normally, so learning to ride was a challenge. Every day I got on the bike and stopped anyone, anywhere, to help me pedal and balance without falling. When I managed two or three turns of the wheels, I felt like I was on a high wire, performing great feats.

I was a bird in flight. I was bewildered by the open

spaces. My new world was a world of balance, speed, and motion: the poplars moving in the wind, weeping willow branches swimming in the pond, tall manicured grasses swaying, geese and swans paddling in the water. I looked at the beautiful Bavarian countryside, at the swift clouds in the gray-blue sky, the birds flying south. I relished being part of Nature and was happy that I, and my hair, was also flying. I pedaled hard, determined to master my new German machine. The wind carried me. I pedaled harder and harder, straighter and straighter, and with each motion, pushed away fear and anger, death, the barn, Demko and Maronka, Zloczów, even my down pillow and comforter.

The next time Frau Doktor came for the piano lesson was a cold and windy day. I was fidgety and restless, but it was too cold and windy to be on the street. I waited for her in the house and loaded our little stove so full with wood that it was shooting sparks and shining bright red. She finally appeared, complaining of the heat. Mother was out on errands, and I was alone. We started by repeating the scales and then practicing Frau Doktor's pride and joy, Für Elise, which we were preparing for the student recital. I couldn't stand it. I felt helpless in front of this army sergeant drilling her charge.

German soldiers again! Her body gave off a terrible odor;

her face perspired. My eyes flew from her sweaty red face to the cuckoo clock above the piano as I counted the minutes. Finally, we were done. After first telling me that I would never learn the piano properly, she carefully wrote down instructions for the next assignment. I curtsied as always, Frau Doktor gathered her music, wiped her face with a handkerchief, and left.

I no longer cared about the cold. There was still plenty of daylight and plenty of time before mother came back, so I loaded the stove again and jumped on my bicycle. I had mastered the balancing problem and rode more easily and for longer distances than ever before. Transported by the brisk wind, I flew faster than the birds. I was proud to be going such a long way from our apartment.

Suddenly I heard a fire engine and saw the military police speeding to our place. I followed the engine only to find out that I had set the piano in our little apartment on fire! Some furniture, the carpet, and paintings my father was collecting were drenched with water and ruined. The bedroom where mother kept our baggage for America was fine, but it reeked with smoke. Mother returned from town with our visas and was very upset. She delivered an angry, painful spanking. She hadn't hit me since the war began, but I was brave, didn't cry, and helped open all the windows. We would be leaving for Deh-Lan-Sey Street in America very soon, and I would never have to have another piano lesson with Frau Doktor Knopf.

THE EYES ARE THE SAME / *174*

16
SS ERNIE PYLE

"**T**HE NEXT SAILING on the *Ernie Pyle* will be from Bremerhaven in two weeks. We have your guarantee, and you'll have your papers by then." The lady from HIAS gave my father more forms and papers and smiled. I also smiled gratefully at her. We are going to America! Each day is more beautiful than the last! The days skip by, an hour is just a flash. No one is more alive than I! I am going on a wonderful journey! America became the center of all my dreams and speculations. I was silent and big-eyed because I was in the midst of a tremendous adventure.

We were leaving the continent on which we had endured so much misery and were sailing for America, New York,

Delancey Street, and my Uncle Isaac. Just before our departure from Deggendorf, we received a parcel from Uncle, real proof of his American wealth. Hysterical with excitement, elation, and triumph, I slashed through the string and began to pull out such wonders as nylon slips and a nylon nightgown for my mother, form-fitting Jockey underwear for my father, at which we are all aghast, and best of all, a beautiful frilly blue nylon dress, gathered at the waist, with white lace trim, just for me. I was the envy of all the kids in our compound, and I preened and danced around in this dress as if I were from America myself!

A long and complicated train journey to the boat ensued—hours past countryside and buildings destroyed by war, and two changes of trains. I paid little attention to the dim landscape—the towns, the locomotive, the signals, the bells, the telegraph masts, and the poles flying by outside. The engine wheels ground rhythmically, speeding along the tracks. A tune went through my head, "A-*me*-ri-ca, A-*me*-ri-ca." So at last I was going to America! Really, really going, at last! Boundaries burst. The arch of heaven soared. A million suns shone out of every star. Winds rushed in from outer space, roaring in my ears, "America! America!" Only the conductor's glistening visor and whistle gently reminded me of earlier trains, of waiting with Olga for Grandfather Mendel. But memory is sometimes kind, and I was able to let go.

Now, I was interested only in our sea voyage and the sea, and was preoccupied with military ships, water, and the harbor we were headed for. I asked endless questions. Does the boat have bells? How many times do they ring before the boat leaves? Can the ship turn around, or does it just swim backward?

I'd studied geography with my father before the trip. We had memorized continents and oceans, cut and pasted them at random on the floor, and I'd played hopscotch jumping from continent to continent. We'd also talked a lot about the history of continents and oceans. I saw the vast blue seas between Europe and America, and I knew I couldn't just skip over continents. Still, I never grasped the special distances, and never understood the cultural and emotional expanse I was about to traverse.

Moving up the Weser River toward the sea, passengers gradually fell silent. They were leaving their native lands, their mother continent, probably never to return. As long as land was in sight, they stood on deck immobilized, struggling to blot out their wartime past.

The *SS Ernie Pyle* pulled away. The foghorn emitted its

lowing, *shofar* sound, and I was a reborn ocean traveler! I was twelve, and my appearance and new identity were very important. I had to dress and groom to regain a sense of self. No more cast-off rags and dresses! I came on board in my new blue-nylon and white-lace dress, and white patent leather Mary Janes that Mother was lucky enough to buy in the flea market in town. They were children's shoes and not at all fashionable, but since my feet were small, they fit well and matched the lace. I also carried a green loden coat, a cast-off, heavy thing, not at all festive—but I didn't care. I was going to America and would hide it away in my bunk as soon as I got the chance.

The *Ernie Pyle*, a military ship operated by the U.S. Military Sea Transportation Service, our cargo of hope, and built to transport 3,000 GIs, carried fewer than six hundred displaced persons. We came on board in Bremerhaven—only a hundred and fifty families (units of more than two), many aged, and sixty-three orphans. There were no facilities for quartering families together. The men bunked aft and the women forward, with cabins reserved for the aged and mothers with small children.

As soon as the ship pulled out of the harbor, I was on deck watching the action and exploring the ship's interiors in near feverish excitement. I got so wild with play that I forgot all fear. I didn't know what came over me, but I couldn't keep still and was impatient for now. During the war, there was no such thing as next time. Tomorrow might never come, so whatever I had to do, it had to be now. I didn't want to stay near my parents more than I had to. I sulked, became stubborn and bossy, and picked fights with other children. America didn't frighten me, but the ocean did. I already knew about large expanses of land—Ukraine, Poland, Czechoslovakia, Germany—but never water. My grandmother once told me that, when the Jews were supposed to cross water, the waves parted miraculously. The waters of the Atlantic did not part for us this time. I was on a huge boat, and there were no miracles. Even in the bunker under the barn, my feet were planted on firm ground. I was programmed to run, to flee and change locations, but here at sea, I was cast adrift and had to depend on the course of the ship. I was also trapped by the perils of the sea. How could I feel safe on a ship if something menacing happened and I had to run away? If there was an *Aktion* here, then what? But I read somewhere that the eternal sea is the only place that guarantees freedom! How could that be? I was befuddled and felt a little seasick.

But there was nothing dull about being on a ship. Everything around me seemed elegant and sparkling and American. In the dining room I got foods I'd never seen before—olives and bananas and oranges, and even pineapple for dessert. I also heard that, in America, great things were endlessly available, everything you could ever want—cars, dollars, strapless dresses, chewing gum, ballpoint pens.

I stood in the prow of the ship, watching the water tear away, forever repeating, forever receding. For days, there was nothing but sea. The Atlantic was so immense, so without end, that I was terrified, happy, and dizzy. Its vastness produced awe, peace, and restlessness, all at the same time.

The crossing was long and rough. The ocean raged and seethed. The sea groaned, and the ship heaved and turned, pitched and rolled. Mountains of black water crowned with foam surrounded us. My heart was like the storm at sea. Night covered the world. I feared that the ocean would swallow our boat, and I awaited our watery grave. Huge billows were forever changing their shapes, slamming against each other in fury, seething and foaming in their anger. I imagined myself alone on the ocean, conscious only of the sea and the sky.

When the storm subsided, the large deck vents were still

emitting nauseating smells and fumes, and I became terribly seasick. I could not be tempted by the beautiful oranges and bananas, and heaved constantly. The torments forced me to live on salt crackers and Coca-Cola. I was ashamed that I couldn't hang around at the Coke machine with the other kids. The machine miraculously dispensed nickel Cokes in bottles. Although the coins jangled in my pockets, I couldn't stand up. Sometimes I felt better and rested on deck in a kind of marine rocking chair. The sun shone on my back. Sometimes a cooling breeze came from the sea, and I felt calmer, more confident that I was going to make it to the other side.

Early on the tenth day, our ship approached New York harbor. I was completely pale and worn out and avoiding the ruddy faced, healthy kids, was up on deck. It was a misty, soft, gray July morning. The first sighting of the Statue of Liberty generated animated conversation, laughter, and tears as people got a peek of the Promised Land. Although the boat turned in the harbor, the Statue of Liberty stared at me all the time, her colossal figure sending a massive and powerful welcome. Fireboats sent up streams of water, and blaring whistles greeted us in a crescendo of sounds. Excited and surprised, my father shouted, "Look! New York is welcoming us!" It was the first time since the war that I had seen him smile.

The ship slowed. I felt a light breeze on my forehead, and as we approached the waterfront, Manhattan rose higher and higher before us out of the sun-shot morning mists. The *SS Ernie Pyle* was dressed up for her arrival. Her flags fluttered from bow to stern, reciprocating New York's greeting. Amidships, eleven foreign flags had been hoisted, including the Polish, Czech, Latvian, Estonian, Romanian, and Hungarian ones. Besides the families and sixty-three orphans, we had a seven-week infant and a seventy-nine-year-old woman. Important officials of the nation, state, and city welcomed us at the pier—eager future citizens of the golden land of milk and honey. Playing "Yankee Doodle Dandy," a waiting brass band also greeted us. There were messages from President Truman and Governor Dewey, and Mayor O'Dwyer spoke for the people of New York.

Our first New York day was soft and gray at first, but it soon turned hot, humid, and very long. We waited on deck, perspiring in our best clothes, suitcases and parcels beside us, ready to disembark. From the deck, we could see groups of people waving, gesticulating, and shouting. We waited and waited for the immigration officials and staff to process our arrival. Finally, with a brilliant red sunset behind us, we were ready to go. My free spirit suddenly abandoned me and I clutched my father's jacket and made sure my mother was right behind me as we walked down the steps to the pier.

Suddenly, from a crowd, we hear a shout, "Yetka! Yetka!" We know that Uncle Isaac has spotted us. He and my mother had not seen each other for twenty-five years, but their genes recognized each other. Their discovery was spontaneous and immediate. They fly into each other's arms and hug for a very long time, sometimes smiling but mostly looking at each other, nodding, and quietly crying. They speak in Yiddish, which left me out, but I am happy to be grounded, standing on firm American soil, feeling New York.

The city is bewildering, strange, complex, and delightfully unexplored. I inhale the clattering tempo of its life, its big unstoppable streets flowing with people and cars, the asphalt sidewalks, the lights, the billboards. Nothing stands still. Everything is running. Giant factory chimneys send up smoke. I close my eyes and listen to the sounds of our new life. They are strange and powerful, as if some hurdy-gurdy rolls had gotten mixed up with pounding music that was stimulating, sometimes ugly, but never false.

"This is America. Life here is very important, very

important," my uncle says, and I giggle and laugh—for the first time since the bunker, I think.

Uncle Isaac goes to find his car while we wait and wait with our baggage. The wait is endless for a now child. Finally, he returns with a very large gray Buick, and we pack in. I am squashed in the front seat between Isaac and my mother, while my father is in the back with the packages and suitcases. As we pull out onto an avenue, I fall quiet, desperately trying to formulate my first American sentence.

"Is this your taxi?" I finally ask. Isaac smiles.

"No, Shoshana, don't be a greenhorn!"

I bristle at my Polish name and the word "greenhorn." Doesn't he know that I am already Susan?

"Here, the yellow-and-black cars you see are called taxis, and they carry passengers from place to place. But my Buick is my own car. I worked, bought it for dollars, and it belongs to me. In America, it is no disgrace to work hard. Workmen and capitalists are equal. Everyone is called 'you' or 'mister,' and everyone goes to school. Education is free. Light is free. Music is free."

I feel comfortable in Isaac's Buick. I have come on wings of irony and fate, the winds of happenstance, and the backs of American machines. I leaped and ran and climbed and crawled; and I would unravel the tangle of events that make up the first breathless years of my American life.

17
IN AMERICA

IT IS A HOT DAY IN AUGUST, in
Brooklyn. "Humidity" is the new word I am learning. "It's
not the heat, it's the humidity," people are saying as I try to
figure out the difference between the two. I know dry strong
northern heat, but this sticky, steamy dampness that makes
my clothes cling and my armpits give off a sultry, unpleasant
smell is completely different.

I wonder if I am really the new me in America as I sit on
the stoop of our small apartment house in Williamsburg. I
am alone and feel very small and a little bit lost as I watch
ladies socializing and kids playing. Pale green trees cover my
side of the street, and I'm hoping that the shaded stoop

makes me invisible.

For a moment I am convinced that the American Susan that came off the SS *Ernie Pyle* had been left on the docks, and that the old Szanka—who feels off center, doesn't speak the language, is dressed differently, and doesn't know about life in America—is sitting here.

I am overcome by a strange faintness as the wet, heavy air wraps itself around me. I can hear the beating of my heart, and for the first time feel its comforting presence. My body is in a state of happy melancholy. My limbs feel heavy, my blood beats fast against the thin skin of my wrists and temples. After years of pain and constriction, there is no fear or darkness anymore. The fetters have been removed at last. Suddenly, I jump on my bike, stretch out my arms on the handlebars and, like a young bird attempting to fly, soar to our new business around the corner.

After a few weeks with Uncle Isaac, HIAS found us an apartment in Williamsburg, and distant American relatives financed a small store for my parents just down the block, the Driggs Avenue Grocery.

Mr. Seltzer, who was soon retiring, agreed to sell his store to my parents, with the provision that he would stay for a while and teach them how to run the grocery. He taught them how to take inventory, how to stock the shelves efficiently, how to negotiate the best prices with food salesmen, where to display the fresh baked goods and "three-for-ten-cents" bagels, and when to run sales for beer. My parents were overwhelmed by the language, the customers, and the salesmen who descended on them like a swarm of flies. Many of Mr. Seltzer's old customers needed to continue their credit and pay once a week, though the salespeople wanted money right away. Mother told her relatives that she knew the grocery business from her father's warehouse in Zloczów. She worked like a horse from dawn to eight at night serving customers and hauling large boxes of cans, soda, and milk bottles. She also prepared meals in the small kitchen in back of the store and never failed to prepare a variation of my comfort food—noodles with milk, now Americanized to spaghetti with cottage cheese and ketchup.

She managed everything. She waited on the customers, added up the prices on a big brown paper bag with a thick black pencil, inquired about their health, and saw them out of the store with a big smile and a personal thank-you. A savvy businesswoman, she prided herself on never making a mistake in her calculations. She didn't miss an opportunity to tell her clients that she was a university graduate, that only the catastrophe of the war in Europe had brought her family here.

My father sat immobilized behind the monumental cast-iron cash register, taking cash or credit while treating customers with the condescension that comes naturally to those who once occupied a higher station in life. He didn't adapt to the grocery business at all and hid in the chair, depressed. He stroked his chest and studied English by reading the newspapers and looking in the dictionary. He complained of angina and a weak heart and rubbed his left side to calm a phantom pain. He was filled with an appalling grief. Images of life before the war—his family, the house, the garden, the country—remained with him forever. He tried to get work as a civil engineer but had a hard time finding a job and so sat in the store, depressed, dreaming of his life in pre-war Poland. The doctor diagnosed his condition as "melancholia," which had at one time been thought of as an illness.

Mr. Seltzer felt bad for him, and would always give him a pep talk. "Forget about your Polish forests and your engineering, Gerson! Hitler took care of everything, and they don't want you back there anyway. This is America, and we must all work hard for our living."

Mr. Seltzer showed him how to calculate prices on specials, open cartons, and stack cans on shelves. Luckily, most cans had tantalizing photographs of the product on the label, so my parents quickly learned how to buy and organize their stock. Indeed, America was a miracle for the housewife: one-stop shopping! She had to visit only one store to prepare an entire meal from the pictures on colorful cans! The Bernice Food salesman was also my father's mentor and would occasionally stop by to chat in Yiddish or instruct him in the finer points of the grocery business while recounting Horatio Alger tales.

"Gerson, wake up, you are in America! You are so lucky to be here, you should kiss the ground! This is a land of opportunity, brains, and *chutzpah*. You've got to hustle. I know a greenhorn who came from Poland only last year and made a fortune marinating and marketing Polish pickles. He's now a millionaire living on Long Island."

Father was energized and animated listening to these tales, but his enthusiasm evaporated as soon as the salesman left, and sadness again overcame him. He was consumed by loneliness. I listened, but I didn't understand. "Millionaire" was one of those fairy-tale words that had no meaning to me, like "emigration" or "naturalization."

Since my parents were working constantly, I was alone most of the time. There wasn't much conversation or physical contact. After Janek and Babcia perished—vanished—Mother, who had first clung too closely to me for life, was now too numbed or too afraid to endure much physical contact. Death had nearly engulfed us. Maybe she was afraid of new losses, afraid to pass on what was inside. She had to survive by working hard for us. I was confused by her withdrawal. I couldn't rescue my parents from their grief and mourning and so retreated into my own exile of survival. I had no cousins, aunts, or uncles, no grandparents, no siblings, no friends. My parents knew other greenhorns from Poland who had settled in New York, but we never visited them. They had settled in better neighborhoods and pretended to continue their pre-war life in Poland. We had landed in a slum, and the grocery business was nothing to brag about. My mother was enslaved by that grocery on Driggs Avenue. Nothing was free in America except the little samples the salesmen passed around. I concluded that what we had been told in Germany and on the boat had been a lie.

What was I to do? I had no choice but to invent another life that would better suit me and my parents. After they left for the grocery store at the crack of dawn, I pulled the covers over my head and fantasized a different routine for them. After all, destiny owed them a more gentrified lifestyle. After Mother's morning coffee, I dressed her in a smart summer suit and spectator shoes, and she would leave with books for English classes. Sometimes she would leave supper for us as she went to meet friends for a concert or a lecture. At other times she would meet her old friends for lunch and a matinee. No more sloppy, flowered housedresses that exposed her brassiere straps and dirty white aprons.

I reinvented my father as his old self, handsome and well dressed. Outfitted in three-piece suits and wearing Brooks Brothers shirts, and flawlessly knotted Sulka or Tripler bow ties, he would leave the apartment each morning for midtown with a beautiful leather briefcase full of important papers. Already a well-known civil engineer in Manhattan, he worked for United States Steel, no less. I carefully cultivated these lies and recounted them to other kids and grown-ups when I left the neighborhood for weekends at my cousin Frieda's house in Bensonhurst. Frieda, a school principal and a distant cousin with no children of her own, took me under her wing to teach me about life in America.

There was no doubt about it. After the passage across the Atlantic, I was more disoriented, less confident, less attractive, less graceful, less fun. I was a somewhat pitiful pale specimen with thick eyebrows, dull, curly hair with no bounce, and dressed in clothes that had nothing to do with current fashions. But Frieda believed in my potential, and she energetically set out to eliminate my flaws. She took me to her house every weekend to teach me how things were done in this country. She initiated me into the mysteries of using shampoos and lotions, putting my hair up in curlers, and applying Ponds and Noxzema night cream when going to bed.

"If you were my daughter, you'd soon look like a princess," Frieda said, suggesting in an undertone that it was time I started wearing a bra.

Cousin Frieda cared for me with more attention and tenderness than my own parents could. Her husband Fred took me fishing and to the beach. They sometimes took me to restaurants and encouraged me to ride the bike and seek out friends in their neighborhood. There, I could spin fabulous tales to new friends about my royal ancestors in Poland, and brag about Europe, a continent they didn't know existed. But they weren't impressed, hadn't a clue about my pedigree, and amused themselves by trading baseball cards and attending ball games at Ebbetts Field.

We devoted Saturdays to shopping in Macy's or Klein's or Ohrbach's. The *profusion* of things—leather purses, rayon blouses, sweetish perfumes, lipsticks, masses of scarves, crinolines, dresses —in these huge palaces of consumerism had me bewildered and very excited. I spent endless hours trying on pretty things in wrong sizes, just to see how they looked. Crushed by this abundance, I came out angry and hostile, pale and depleted. Since I had no money and cousin Frieda was not forthcoming, I made a conscious decision to stop wanting. I couldn't buy anything, and if I were to continue wanting, there would be no end to my deprivation. I forced myself to withdraw and become indifferent. I walked as if I had a steel rod running down the middle of my back and could pass between the taffeta dresses and silk lingerie without feeling temptation. I trained myself to become immune to envy and desire. It wasn't genuine, I knew, and under the feigned serenity and detachment, a cauldron of regret and rage kept seething.

I turned over a new leaf. I began to concentrate on my internal spiritual goods instead. In school, I could really learn the language and read important books on everything in the library. I used Frieda as my educational consultant on weekends. She suggested what books to read and taught me not to plagiarize articles from the encyclopedia for school reports I showed her.

"You didn't write this!"

"Yes, I did. It's my handwriting. See?" My pronunciation was getting better but still wasn't flawless like Lowell Thomas's on the radio.

"No, I mean, you aren't using your own words. 'Eschew'? 'Altruistic'? 'Enterprise'? 'Flawed'? 'Fragile premises'?"

"What do you mean?"

"I mean you took this straight out of the encyclopedia!" she scolded.

"Yes, the *World Book* is a very nice encyclopedia. It has very good articles. My teacher said I should use it, so I went to the library and wrote this report."

Frieda was upset. "You can't copy the whole article, word for word, and turn it in as your report. It's too easy, and it's wrong. It's called plagiarism. Try to find your own words. Always use your own words. Didn't you ever write reports?"

"No, I never went to school in Poland. My father taught me to read from newspapers."

She became calm. "Well, you should always use your own words in a report. You can research facts in encyclopedias and books, but always use your own words, and find your own way of saying things."

Cousin Frieda spoke differently from others. Her sentences were vigorous and round, and she finished with just the right point, with assurance and self-control. Very early I figured out that speech is a class signifier, that most people slurred their words, stumbled, or repeated the same phrases too many times, in sentences that trailed off aimlessly. It was important for me to speak well, and I learned quickly. Every day I learned new words, new expressions, new rhythms of speech. I picked them up from Frieda, from my teachers, from conversations, from books.

"Shudd-*up*" was the first English word I understood in its dramatic context. I didn't like the expression "you're welcome," and could hardly bring myself to say it. For me it implied there was something requiring gratitude, which in Polish would be impolite. There were words I learned from books whose sound I loved, and I was sure I really understood their meaning. Some words, like "enigmatic" or "insolent," had only a literary value at first and existed only as signs on a page, but I could make a living connection and eventually use them in a book report.

Rebuilding connections between picture and word in a new language is daunting. My old interior language was vanishing, and with it its interior images, while new English words didn't hook onto anything. Slowly I processed the new meanings. The new language was mine, all mine. I bought it word for word on credit, with hard work, the American way. The English language owned me, too. I began to think in it, and even dream in it. I was quickly losing my accent, but sometimes when I got angry or tired, something funny happened to the cadence of my speech and the way I pronounced some words like "eschew" as "ess-*cue*".

Finally it is Sunday evening and I am home on South Second Street. It's nice to be able to undress in my little room in front of a mirror, stroke my hips, and examine how my breasts are growing. They are round and white and crowned with tingly pink tips and make me feel sultry and warm. They are still hard to notice under a sheer blouse, and maybe I do need a brassiere. I get into a cool nightgown, robe, and slippers, and my parents and I sit down to watch the enlightening and educational Ed Sullivan Show on our little television set, a house gift from Uncle Isaac.

A summer breeze blows through the venetian blinds and ruffles the curtains, and I feel content. There is no fear here in America. I feel both love and sadness for Mother and Father, because I cannot change their life, so full of drudgery, or rescue them from the grief that sometimes engulfs them. But if I read a lot, study, pronounce words correctly, and learn to write reports with my own words, my life will be different, they will be proud of me, and I might even become a principal like cousin Frieda!

Suddenly, while watching Ed Sullivan, I feel a warm trickle down my thigh and see blood marking a narrow red path down my bare leg. I am alarmed! Something mysterious is happening. Without warning, blood is flowing from my own body. Old fears return. I feel alone and naked. Mother senses my panic and understands. She picks me up in her strong arms, carries me to my soft white bed, and kisses my forehead, mouth, and eyes for a long, long time. As I am returning to a half-forgotten childhood, she hugs me, whispering, "Darling, now you're a woman." I quietly rejoice in our secret celebration, sharing bonds of adulthood and womanhood with my mother, in America.

AFTERWORD
RETURNING TO POLAND

"No whiteness lost
is so white
as the memory of whiteness."
—William Carlos Williams

BETWEEN 1934, the year I was born, and 1945, the Nazis killed six million Jews and systematically destroyed the flourishing Jewish communities of Europe. When the war ended, my family and I also suffered a complete break with our past. My center collapsed, and with it any sense of security, identity, and rootedness. All continuity—provided by community, extended family, and surroundings—irretrievably vanished. My world was shaken to its foundations. The immediate past was too horrible to contemplate, the childhood past before the war too irrelevant and too difficult to remember.

After the killing was over, we fled Poland and put thousands of miles between us and what used to be home, in the hope of never seeing or remembering again. We fled into visions of a better present and future, knowing that any future would be better than the past. Friends and acquaintances made up for uncles and grandmothers no longer there.

Although real memory was a desert, I remembered viscerally and with my heart, almost always in a state of anxiety, almost always with subliminal expectation of catastrophe. And yet, I wanted to return. I wanted to confront the tragedy of my childhood. And I did return—first to Zloczów, then to Warsaw, ostensibly to attend a Children of the Holocaust meeting. I wanted to understand how some Polish "children of the Holocaust," those who chose to remain in Poland after the war, were managing life without a usable past.

In America, thoughts of Poland were always associated with a feeling of insanity in my head. I wanted to keep my feelings at bay and to see Poland as completely foreign. But I was pulled by my past. Returning sixty years later, I was convinced that the insanity was going to be real. But I decided to retrace a trail of reminiscences and memories, which I had never dared disturb before. Certain memories returned unexpectedly. Fragmentary scenes that had haunted me in the past now obsessed me: my little brother Janek, perhaps abandoned by my grandmother on the doorsteps of a nunnery, now sixty-five and forever searching for us in Poland, Venezuela, America, or Israel.

I first flew to Kyiv, the capital of Ukraine, anxious to take the train to L'viv and Złoczów before the meeting in Warsaw. I wanted to return to my town, my birthplace, the streets, shops, parks, river, my grandmother's house, and the many wonderful vacation spots I had visited. I was determined to dream again and learn to trust the past. Mourning and searching for my lost childhood, for that damaged child that survived the Nazi genocide, I expected to come back to a country that had been frozen for decades in my past, but which was now inhabited by living people whose faces would be both lovely and dreadful.

What happened next was a shock.

I felt as if nothing evil had ever happened there. No more the child looking for unrequited love, I discovered that I was actually at peace with myself. When I first saw the beauty of the countryside, my early years reappeared. Poland—now Ukraine—was the same, but I was different. Meadows and forests beckoned. The countryside unrolled like the canvas of a naïve painting come to life.

The countryside's flat, monotonous, and pre-industrial feel was exciting to me. Some of it looks like a tourism poster. There was the a flaxen-haired, pig-tailed, blue-eyed, pug-nosed little girl standing in front of a picture-book cottage in a picture-book garden filled with marigolds, mallow, daisies, hollyhocks, phlox, and nicotiana, all in bloom. There were also the small unkempt houses, barns with corrugated roofs, the not quite picture-postcard pretty roads and alleys dotted with roadside shrines. And the religious kitsch, plastic flowers, painted figures of the Virgin and Child, icons in glass frames, and figures of the bleeding Jesus, nails driven through palms, a crown of thorns, a martyred Jew.

White clouds sailed across a light blue sky and the countryside turned to tall grasses and wildflowers and shade trees that trembled in the slight movement of air. As the train approached L'viv, geese and chickens scattered in the fields. Roosters crowed and farm animals jabbered. The harmony of the countryside was enthralling: flat meadows dotted by round, narrow haystacks with poles shaped like inverted ice cream cones, farmyards and rivers, the air smelling of flowers and hay, clumps of birch trees, ponds, tumbledown farmyard cottages with unkempt thatched roofs. I saw meadows filled with poppies and blue cornflowers, orchards laden with red and yellow cherries, and white geese pecking at a green slope! My train crossed country roads and brilliant wheat fields near gardens with blazing sunflowers; it passed a canopied forest, always following a ribbon of silvery river that glittered among the trees in the distance. I was excited by the vistas and sounds from my childhood that I could never find elsewhere. It was a dream come true! If I unearthed my childhood dreams, I could become a child again, return to that sheltered time of fun and peace expunged from my life long ago but not quite dead and buried. The forgotten language that I spoke as a child also reemerged. Childhood was an echo, a muted incomprehensible murmur, and I was jubilant when I could put sentences together and be understood.

I took the train directly east, first stopping in L'viv. I tried to resurrect feelings of my parents' nostalgia and romance for Lwów but couldn't. For half of its eight-hundred-year history it had been Polish and, along with Kraków, the pride of that country. But now the city embodied poverty in grandeur. The grand old shops in the old "Vienna of the

East" were either gone or were now selling leather jackets, pants and shirts from Southeast Asia. Every second building was a self-important financial center with shabby exchange offices, all offering identical rates. Crowds of babushkas lined lovely old cobbled streets, patiently selling bags of cherries or bunches of flowers.

More of the romance and excitement dissipated on the long and wearying train trip from L'viv to Zloczów, now Zolochiv. I stared out the window, reading signs of towns that didn't seem familiar at all. Finally, we neared my goal; the train began to lose speed and came to a halt at the far end of the platform. I looked through the window at a sign in Ukrainian, resembling a cinematic close-up:

ZOLOCHIV—CENTER OF THE
TELEVISION INDUSTRY IN UKRAINE

The decaying town was the product of bureaucratic planning. I saw green, Soviet-style concrete apartment buildings with a sea of television aerials on rooftops, lopsided windows, and balconies used as storerooms, with laundry flapping in the breeze. The old train station had also changed. The large stone balls on either side of the wide steps were gone. Droshkies had once waited there in the dappled light to ferry passengers across the meadows between the town and the station. Now, an enterprising young woman was selling Chinese T-shirts and Indian purses as I waited for a Lada taxi to arrive. The persistent echoes of the past quickly faded when I spotted a line of freight cars along the tracks and remembered the barbed wire that had covered the small openings in the sides of wagons long ago. Another modern addition, the kiosk, was closed for *remont*. A dusty window displayed two tired blouses, two pairs of cheap sunglasses, some plastic hair barrettes in the shape of bows, and a T-shirt stenciled LVIV, with the old castle in the background.

My genial cabbie was thrilled to have a foreign tourist as his passenger. Tall and lanky, he barely fit into the driver's seat. His red American baseball cap, small horn-rimmed glasses, and well-groomed tufts of beard suggested he was the intellectual he pretended to be. My pastiche of Polish and Russian somehow passed for broken Ukrainian as we conversed about the town while he complained about the lack of tourists. As we approached the hotel, he became more formal and announced, in the manner of a tourist guide: "Hotel Zolochiv, category three-star."

The hotel had been designed in the put-up-cheap-and-fast style of Khrushchev's urban planning. A white concrete rectangle, seven stories high and with boxy windows, the Hotel Zolochiv sported a freshly varnished oak front door decorated with brass moldings and a large plastic bouquet of wheat stalks. The lobby was deserted. A pretty girl behind the reception counter welcomed me with a special Slavic blend of charm and style. Her bright pink dress, earrings, lipstick, and fingernails underscored a pleasant manner that made me feel at home. When I gave her a make-up case with eye shadow from America as a small gift, she was ecstatic.

I told her I had been born on Pilsudski Street, now called Shevchenko, near the old square, and was interested in finding older natives who might have known my family. She began in tourist-book English, "I welcome you with friendship and hospitality," but then lapsed immediately into Ukrainian. "You know, my father has lived here all his life. When Zolochiv was Polish, he built apartment houses for Jews. When the Germans occupied the town, he became a Volksdeutscher and supervised road construction for the *Wehrmacht*. When the Russians came, he worked for the Ministry of Housing.

"My father knew everyone in the old town. I will bring him to the hotel tomorrow, and he can show you around. He is on pension now and a building consultant for the municipality, but there is no money, and he has little work. When I got my job in the hotel, he decided to help me and my family and do guide work with tourists. He only speaks Ukrainian, Polish, and Russian, but that's OK because we have no tourists from the West."

The bellman and I had trouble squeezing into the small elevator with my large suitcase. My room was not much bigger than the elevator, with scarcely enough space to open the case. A whiff of disinfectant drifted in from an adjoining bathroom with modern plumbing, army-issue toilet paper, and a stained bath. But the room was clean, had the basic comforts, and a phone.

From my window on the sixth floor, I looked out over the new Zolochiv. Architectural banality had robbed the new town of any local character. Anonymous new streets and concrete blocks of houses and factories had nothing to do with my Zloczów. The television industry had become its claim to fame.

I began planning what I would do the next day. I'd get up early, maybe as the sun cast its first slanting light across the meadows, walk the two miles or so to the river, near where the old bridge used to stand, and continue to the main square in the old part of town, where my grandmother's apartment house stands, and where we lived. *Ja pamietam, ja pamietam, tak, tak* (I remember, I remember, yes, yes). That nostalgic refrain hammered like a woodpecker's echo in my head. I wanted the old part of town to unfold slowly, poetically, like time unbuckling, and smell the flowers and hay.

Early next morning, Pan Franko was already waiting in the lobby. For a man in his eighties, he was still muscular and strapping. He wore an East German-made maroon jogging suit. His face was smooth and pleasant, completely wrinkle-free, his hair was curly white. His blue eyes sparkled and blinked nervously as he puffed away on a Marlboro. His nose was pink, probably from too much vodka and high blood pressure. He greeted me with shortened breath and a slight arthritic limp and proudly showed his identification, an old Soviet business card—one side in Russian, the other in Ukrainian. The job description seemed unreal:

Manager of the Architecture and Town Planning Board
DEVELOPMENT AND RECONSTRUCTION
OF THE CITY OF ZOLOCHIV AND ITS SUBURBS

Leaving behind the noisy world of modern Zolochiv, we walked along a peaceful shady avenue where the tarmac, worn away in places, revealed patches of original cobblestone beneath. Here were the first intimations of the old country town. The place still had a provincial feel, small enough to be explored on foot, with views of meadows, fields, and river. Luckily, the new highway bypassed it, keeping heavy traffic away. The old ice cream shop next to the movie house was still there, as were the two stone cherubs with their chubby cheeks. The old square was unchanged. The neoclassical facades remained intact, one with 1860 carved on its pediment. The scale of the old architecture reflected Zloczów's prosperity in the second half of the nineteenth century, and the square retained a measure of dignity in a congeries of buildings and styles from various periods. Pan Franko told me that the municipality has plans for the historic restoration of the square.

Our house stood in the old square. The original wrought-iron railings of my grandmother's balcony were still there, gracing the house and the park below. It was now the region's agricultural bank, the spacious, airy rooms busy with people and computers. Their initial wariness of a Polish-speaking visitor dressed like a foreigner evaporated once I explained to the manager that I'd lived in the building when it was a private home long ago. He showed me around, but the staff paid too much attention to my American pantsuit and Nike walking shoes, and I felt out of place. The director of the bank quickly agreed to guide me through my grandmother's large apartment. His name was Oleksandr Kovalenko, and he was a graduate of the Odessa Institute of Credit and Economy and a former academician of Kyiv University. A short, stocky man in his sixties, he told me he was married, and that his wife and two children lived in Kyiv, where he traveled every weekend.

The ceilings seemed much lower than I remembered, and peeling stucco contributed to the general air of neglect. I felt more uncomfortable remembering my first encounter with death in the enclosed courtyard, where the garden had been as overgrown as it was that day. The old angel fountain was still not working. As I left, I made small talk about Russian fertilizer exports and good harvests, and let myself out the old kitchen door into the courtyard.

Beyond the square, things turned shabby. The old town had been cheapened wherever a new building had replaced the old. The architectural tedium made the place feel stagnant and dull because it no longer had an economic life of its own. Where were the tailors, butchers, the chocolate shop, and all the other shop fronts? Dozens of homes, sharing the fate of their occupants, had been wiped out and replaced by a

new population from the east. Nazi vandalism, years of neglect, uncertainty about ownership, and leaking roofs had all
led to decay. The place had a disjointed, bedraggled look, as
if waiting for another gang to come along and finish the job.
Mr. Franko couldn't wait to get me out of what he considered
the "wretched" part of town and show me something truly
worthy of my "homecoming."

The old synagogue, in rubble fifteen years before, had
recently been restored from old photographs by a wealthy
Złoczówer from Australia. It was prettier than I remembered, glowing white in the gray light. It had a quiet, graceful
presence but lacked any lingering aura of holiness. There was
no one to pray there anymore. Trees in the front courtyard
soared above the roof, their dark trunks silhouetted against
the fresh white stucco. Sometimes, when visiting Złoczów
for the High Holy Days, children played beneath them during the long service. The doors were locked; the place was
silent. The weight of memory lent it a desolate air in spite of
the fresh paint work. Why restore a synagogue in a town
without Jews? Was it a cultural icon? A historical landmark?
A Jewish philanthropic gesture across the oceans from
Australia?

Mournful, muted sounds of horns and trombones drifted

across the road from a music school on the corner of the street. A small street opposite the synagogue had once housed a Jewish slaughterhouse, where Grandmother took her live chickens and where my cousins and I brought our scape-birds on the eve of Yom Kippur. My grandfather whirled a quacking chicken around my head to atone for my sins and chanted the prayers for *kapurah*. This barbaric ritual was sinister and alarming. I panicked each time the bird shrieked. When feathers flew over my head, I thought the world was ending.

Caught up in the past, I meandered on, looking for clues to my present. There were few. I felt a sense of intense loss. Every trace of Jewish life had been expunged. The place denied its past. The *Bes midrosh* next to the synagogue was still recognizable, but, secured by painted metal struts protruding from the red clay roof, a sign revealed that it was now a public library. I was happy that the building still housed books. The small one next to the synagogue, once the *mikva*, was now a bakery. The old newspaper and tobacco shop was now a motor club office. One side of the street where Jewish cloth merchants had had their stores was being demolished by a Caterpillar bulldozer.

I felt unreal, both a grown-up and a child, walking

dreamlike through streets I had walked so many times in my mind. Pan Franko recounted the town's history and plied me with local jokes and anecdotes, but I just wanted to see and remember. He said that he'd known Grandfather Mendel and used to play cards with him. "Yes, unfortunate errors have, no doubt, occurred. There were *bolshiye nepriyat-nosti*." *Unpleasant events*—the words jarred. "The talk abroad is that Poles and Ukrainians murdered Jews," he said, dismissing the charge. "The truth is, many helped Jews. But there were so many informers, and the penalty was death for us and our families. We got on all right with Jews. We did not hate each other." He spontaneously volunteered this view. I neither asked questions nor wanted to examine his conscience.

We walked in the direction of the river, past the Jewish cemetery, a wilderness of graves neglected for years, crumbling and gradually sinking into the ground. It was a scene of devastation, with broken lumps of granite and marble used as building materials for the new sports stadium in the new Zolochiv. At the entrance stood a carved stone memorial to the victims of Nazism. The inscription read:

To the Faithful Sons of the Homeland

MURDERED BY THE NAZI FASCISTS
IN THE YEARS 1939–1945

"Did the citizens of Zolochiv erect a memorial to the Jews who lived among them for five hundred years and been exterminated?" I asked. "Is there a plaque to tell the people of Zolochiv that this was once a holy burial ground?" Pan Franko told me that the Zolochiv local council had recently erected a plaque on the site of the ruined cemetery. He led me to the bronze tablet, which bore the Star of David and the following inscription:

JEWISH CEMETERY, PROTECTED BY LAW.
RESPECT THIS RESTING PLACE OF THE DEAD.

He told me there was another place where more Jews were buried and pointed to a path, far away, leading uphill to the large Catholic cemetery and to a place hard to find. We trudged along in silence. The Catholic cemetery spread across a steep hillside on the outskirts of town, a peaceful place close to the Franciscan monastery. Old chestnut trees shaded the well-tended graves, simple marble crosses, and family tombs. Candles flickered amid bunches of newly laid flowers. There were reminders of the war: monuments to

soldiers who had fallen in battle, civilians who'd been "innocent victims of the Nazi terror." Suddenly, we came upon a
Star of David engraved on a simple tombstone. "This is
where Jewish prisoners from the labor camp Lackie Wielkie
and Sasów were interred," he whispered. Sasów had been
near the place where my father worked for the *Wehrmacht!*
The memorial marking the mass grave was inscribed:

> To the Jews Abominably Murdered
> by the Nazi Oppressors
> in Lackie Wielkie and Sasów
> in the Years 1941–1943

By the time of their deaths, the Jewish cemetery had
already been in ruins. Now, clusters of marigolds not yet in
bloom filled the square space, and the large grave, like others,
was well cared for. Unfortunately, the area next to the
memorial was used as a landfill for rotting leaves, broken
glass, and litter. An old nervous twitch in my neck returned,
and my back stiffened.

I thanked the old man, gave him ten dollars, said good-
bye, promised to send him the American Adidas jogging suit
he requested without embarrassment, and continued to the
river alone. A grassy embankment with dark clumps of weeds

and wildflowers softened the edges of the banks as well as my anxiety. A faint aroma of moss rose from the unsown earth. A lone angler leaned forward, staring at his line. In dappled light, the Zloczówka cast its calming spell. It remained a gently flowing, tranquil river following an unspoiled vista of flat meadowland, just as I remembered. For centuries Jews had come to the river's edge on Rosh Hashana for the annual ceremony of *Tashlich*, to cast their sins upon the waters. I stared at the beauty, smelled the grassy dampness, and remembered. Cows grazed in the foreground. In the distance was a low horizon with an enormous sky. But the illusion of timelessness evaporated when I looked west. A modern steel footbridge had replaced the old wooden one, and trucks spewing fumes thundered on a highway. Electric towers dotted the landscape. The sound of the river only occasionally drowned out the roar of the trucks. I stood by the river's edge and smelled the grass and watched the drops of rain prick the shiny surface of the water. As the rain came down harder, I made my way back to town.

Early the next morning, before going to the station to catch the Warsaw train, I stood at the edge of the new town looking over the meadows toward the old. A little girl was driving a herd of goats in the fields. The morning breeze suggested that there had never been a war. I felt no emotions. Amid this serenity, it was impossible to grasp the horror. Floodgates of old feelings closed. The rain had washed everything clean, leaving the sky a piercing blue. The morning traffic was powerless to pollute so flawless a day. My journey was done, my curiosity had been satisfied, the ache in my heart had been relieved. I did not regret leaving. I felt no emotion. Zloczów was releasing me from its grip, and I was able to move on.

It was a beautiful summer afternoon when I arrived in Warsaw for the annual gathering of the Hidden Children of the Holocaust. Złoczów was far, far away. The sun shone. Scattered clouds sailed lazily across the sky. Birds were singing in fields and gardens. The conference was meeting in Count Ledochowski's estate, a stately old mansion in the leafy suburbs of Warsaw, recently converted to a hotel— white, neoclassical, with a low, sloping gray slate roof and a dozen main rooms arranged on two floors around a central staircase. The rooms were light and elegant, the walls high, with molded ceilings. Large octagonal windows faced a wide lawn in front. The windows in the back overlooked a lake surrounded by a beautiful park with gardens, walks, and fountains. The house was neither imposing nor ostentatious.

It possessed the essence of nobility.

In Soviet times, the place was used as a house of rest for officials from the Ministry of Culture. Bicycle paths, a jogging path around the lake, a volleyball court, and new tennis courts were added then, along with the poplar trees planted by Stalin's urban planners to create "green zones" or "shade in a hurry" in the capitals of the new Soviet empire. At that time, the trees were shedding *"puch"*. When this happens, it looks and feels as if one were walking under a torn-down pillow. The stuff looks and moves like snow and marks the arrival of summer in Warsaw. It makes people sneeze; it floats into eyes, noses, and morning cups of coffee.

Now that Poland is an independent and free country, *puch* elicits no more than a shrug. When I asked a gardener about it, he replied with a political soliloquy, as blue smoke from his cigarette swirled around his face: "We are too weary to notice all the disasters the Soviets brought to this part of the world! Chernobyl, nuclear subs rusting in our fishing grounds in the Baltic, dioxin-laced soot spewing on our towns and villages, drinking water that makes Geiger counters ring. The Communists foisted environmental catastrophes upon our suffering land!"

Olga, a caretaker in the hotel who made extra money

cleaning apartments, soon joined the conversation. Exasperated, she complained, "I hate it. You can try to mop it up with a wet cloth, but afterward it just flies around again. Now, it's just part of nature. We have to put up with it. We blame everything on the Soviets." She turned to the gardener to ask, "Now, please tell me, was *puch* also responsible for Stalin's purges?"

I nodded and smiled and walked down a beautiful wildflower path toward the lake to meet some of the other "children." About two hundred were attending the conference. They were part of the largest hidden children's group in Eastern Europe (eight hundred in all). They had chosen to remain in the center of the cataclysm. They live and work, so to speak, at the scene of the crime. They are mostly retired professionals, low-profile Jews, loyal Polish citizens, proud to be partners in the European Union but wary of Poland's newly gained political and economic freedoms. They have not abandoned their Polish roots and are attached to Polish soil, history, art, and literature. They survived in attics, sewers, bunkers, foundling hospitals, orphanages, on false papers, in monasteries and nunneries. Some were thrown out of cattle cars en route to concentration camps, others into the Vistula River to drown; still others were left on doorsteps.

They were all raised by Catholic families, nurtured by the Catholic religious canon, and learned to practice the Catholic faith. Many have only recently discovered their identity. Inexplicably, Yiddish culture tugged like an undertow on these "Catholic Jews," and as adults, they have come out of hiding. Some are close friends and know each other socially. Sixty years later, old grievances and unresolved ambiguities encourage them to learn about all things Jewish. They feel that only at these gatherings can they be entirely themselves, freely socialize, and learn about Jewish culture and traditions.

The next morning, I attended my first workshop, "Identity and Empowerment: Who Am I?" The title intrigued me. It was run by a second-generation Polish-Jewish psychiatrist, Professor Klinger, a pudgy man with a well-tended mustache and goatee and stylishly round metal-rimmed glasses.

About ten of us sat in a circle, eight women and two men. We took turns explaining our reasons for coming to the workshop. As expected, the introductions were typically Polish: correct academic protocol, formal, very proper, no small talk, no sense of ease, humor, or comfort, and, in some instances, acute embarrassment. It was difficult for me to see how an open discussion of something as fundamental as identity could get going. All began with the "Who am I?" part—with personal histories and tales of survival. Empowerment was secondary.

Bożena, a chemist from Wroclaw, began by telling the group how a farmer on the way to market noticed a bundle wrapped up in a peasant shawl lying in a ditch. He stopped, picked up a one-and-a-half-year-old child, and brought her home. The family was childless, and the child was a miracle, a gift from God. They raised her as their own, loved her, and taught her prayers. One day, three men carrying rifles entered the house. "Where is the child?" they asked. Her Polish mother showed them to the bed where she was sleeping. One of the men knelt, kissed the sleeping child, and said: "We know you will save this child. Please keep on caring for her, and we will repay you."

The man was the child's father, fighting with the Home Army, the Polish nationalist underground. He survived the war. When the Soviet army entered Poland that summer, the same man and a woman arrived to claim the child, but the Polish family did not want to give her back. They fled west with all their property and the child, to a secluded village. But after a while her Jewish parents succeeded in abducting her. When she got older, she found her Polish parents and visited them often. "They felt betrayed and deceived when I was stolen from them," she said. "I loved all four the same. They were all my parents." But her Jewish parents didn't want to know that the others existed, and they never visited them.

"After the liberation, we stayed in Poland," Bożena continued. "I don't know why. My Jewish father was in the Polish army, and my uncle fought for Poland in a Polish uniform. He still had to explain that he had not personally participated in the crucifixion of Christ and had barely escaped from Wroclaw when someone who knew him shouted, 'What are you doing here, you lousy Jew?' Both my parents died and are buried in Poland."

"Why, then, did you stay here? Why, after everything that befell us?" someone asked.

Bożena had been educated at Wroclaw University. She is a professor there and does research in biochemistry. She married a Christian because there were no Jewish men around, but both their children left Poland and settled in Israel. She has a comfortable academic life, travels to seminars in Sweden, Germany, and Norway. "I didn't have the strength to leave. I am one of the few left in this cemetery of Jewish people."

Julek, a jolly, heavy-set man with a cherubic face, was next. "I live part of the time in Jerusalem and part of the time in Kraków. I love Kraków, and I love being in my old neighborhood. We lived on Miodowa Street, near Helena Rubinstein's family. When I return here, time stands still. I'm a teenager and a mischief-maker all over again. I walk all the alleyways and shortcuts in Kaźimierz, and our boys quarrel about our soccer game that afternoon. We play soccer in the courtyard behind the cemetery, and often the ball flies directly to the grave of Rabbi Lazar, the eighteenth-century sage, a real *tzadík*. A beggar is still singing a mournful ballad about the sinking of the Titanic. In the courtyard of the prayer house on Kierków Street, the faithful still gather for prayer, and the cantor intones in his high voice: 'Blessed be Thou our God and the God of our fathers, God of Abraham, God of Jacob, God of Isaac.' Our school, on the corner of Soltyka Street, still stands. To this day, I remember my eighth-grade Latin teacher, Pan Santocki. We used to make fun of his huge, floppy ears and called him Professor Asinus, which of course means donkey. Now, I come home every summer and rent an apartment on Wielicka, near the market. I like all the commotion there, the smell of flowers, fruits, and vegetables. I also love the smell of fresh fish. Before the war, the fishermen would store their fish in crates in the river, and fishmongers sold fresh, live flapping fish right from the same crates. I remember my childhood in Kraków and on my farm like yesterday, and I come for the summer months here, alone, and go back to Jerusalem when they begin selling roasted potatoes from a portable oven in the market. Roasted potatoes were always our first sign of autumn."

Julek spoke as if from a sepia photograph. He was scrupulous about addresses, houses, places, colors, sounds, even smells—memories concealed in the deepest corners of his soul. He painted the landscapes of memory, his pre-war daily life, in unusually sensual terms: Jewish sweat that smelled of garlic and onions; the marketplace redolent of fresh baking, coffee, horse manure, and smoke from factories; and synagogues steeped in the odors of dust and wax.

"My wife, Klara, is also from Kraków, but she doesn't like to come here. She says she doesn't find it interesting and spends her time visiting our daughter in Los Angeles instead. My permanent address is Kraków, but there is a sense of something missing. I still have a few old buddies here. We go to the Klezmer Festival, have a few drinks, and talk about old times. The finest restaurant in Kraków is the Chata, the peasant restaurant. Plenty of vodka, the best homemade rye bread, cut very thick, and *smalec*. I want to live in my country as an equal, not as an enemy or a stranger, but something is missing."

The group grew uncomfortable with so many personal details of Julek's story, but there was no stopping him.

"Why did you come to this workshop, Julek?" Bożena asked. "I don't understand. I am sorry I never left. How can you feel more at home here, especially after the Kielce pogrom? I ask you why no other nation did this to their Jews after the war? Not one."

A woman from the middle of our circle stared at Julek and said angrily, "Aren't you ashamed of yourself? You are an Israeli citizen!"

"Yes, I am a citizen," he replied, "but Israel is not my motherland. I lost my motherland. The Poles and Jews never wanted to know how many great Polish poets were of Jewish origin."

"Everyone here has a schizophrenic attitude toward Poland," grumbled Dr. Klinger.

"Israel is my country," Julek continued, "but I want to spend more time here. Poland is a beloved country, the country I remember from my childhood. I am Polish, but I hate the Poles, especially many of the older ones who murdered and burned our people in the ghetto."

Julek then turned to the psychiatrist. "Doctor, you didn't tell me what to do about my Polish conundrum. I came to this workshop because only here can people understand me. In Los Angeles, my daughter's family is Jewish Orthodox, and they think I'm not a Jew. In Jerusalem, my friends think I'm mad as a hatter."

"Well, you are!" a young blond man, obviously from the second generation, shouted. "You come here with your dollars and pension to have a good time. Your world was here, but it's gone: the hatter's shop, the jeweler's shop, leather goods, textiles, prayer books, and pens. Everyone's gone—the shopkeepers, the restaurant owners, the watchmakers."

The meeting took on a life of its own. The issue was no longer identity and empowerment but our sense of identity in the context of Polish history before and after the Holocaust.

"It's different for me," a much older woman volunteered. "I come from a Polonized background. I was raised on Polish literature, in the Polish language. But why should you love Poland so dearly?"

Another elegant lady, with an aristocratic Polish face, graying hair in a bun, and a long string of sumptuous pearls,

chimed in. "My family fled to Uzbekistan in 1941. We registered as Polish nationals. My parents worked in a metal mine.
We survived on soup and potatoes. Father taught me the
alphabet from a Mickiewicz poetry book. For us, Poland is an
aching wound. Our Polish brothers were evil, but Poland our
mother was good." She fidgeted with her pearls and remained
silent for the remainder of the session.

"Please, go on with the introductions," Prof. Klinger said,
and pointed to me.

"I am part of a large group of Hidden Children living in
America. There was too much pain here. Our family was
killed, we were expelled. We left with bitterness, but we were
happy to leave the Polish graveyard. I feel at home in
America. Here, people say they are at home, but I feel foreign. My Polish is very rusty. I never have to hide my
Jewishness in America. I decided to return for this meeting
because I wanted to heal more wounds with Polish landscapes, with weeping willows, the aroma of Polish woods, and
pierogi with blueberries. It's been a very long time."

I was embarrassed by my stabs at humor and my unre-
fined and ungrammatical Polish. The fact that I was also a
hidden child seemed irrelevant. I was a stranger. Here,
among the Poles, I was only an intrusive and curious

American, and many in the group spent more time assessing my clothes than listening. Finally, a well-dressed lady sitting next to me commented quietly and sarcastically. "You only suffer from nostalgia. You are a tourist in this world."

"And you?" I asked.

"I live here. We who live here really suffer."

Wojtek was next. He looked younger than many of us. He was very quiet and shy, and had sad blue eyes. He began to speak, looking directly at Julek. "You are so lucky to be able to return to Kraków, to know who your parents were and where you lived. I was not even two years old when my grandmother brought me to a convent before she was taken to a concentration camp. She brought me to the nunnery and disappeared.

"I cried and cried for my grandmother and mother all the time. The sisters taught me all the prayers to help me find my mother. There were other children in the convent, but I was circumcised, and the nuns had to hide me when the police came for inspections. I prayed and prayed for a kind, mythical creature looking like Mother Superior to come and claim me. I sat on the cold floor of the chapel, peeing and dirtying myself, tears and snot sliding down my cheeks, crying all the time. When I came out of the chapel, Sister Teresa always had a little bag of sugar for me to suck, and prayed with me. She told me that my grandmother had tried to keep me but couldn't. She'd told her that she escaped with me from Zloczów, a town near Lwów. I was baptized and raised as a Catholic. Sister Teresa explained that, since I was abandoned, I was now the property and trust of the church, and only the church was responsible for my wellbeing.

"It was only two years after liberation that Jewish charities, and Israeli officials, came looking for abandoned Jewish children and took me to an orphanage with other abandoned Jewish children. Who am I? I was baptized, but my parents circumcised me as a Jew. Sister Teresa said I went through the rites of passage twice. I hated the orphanage and missed the sisters, who had prayed with me and given me sugar and white bread with jam. We were moved to another orphanage that was much worse. In the yard, the older boys kicked us and beat us. They woke us at night, made us get out of bed and told us the place was inhabited by hobgoblins, demons, dybbuks, and devils. I believed them and often woke up in a wet bed.

"That orphanage was near a train station, and every Sunday afternoon, groups of people would come off the train, looking for their children. We had to be neatly dressed, holding hands, and smiling. We greeted the groups searching for lost children. We were always smiling. Each time someone looked very carefully at us, we ran to them thinking they were our parents or relatives. Once I was sure I saw my mother coming to claim me, but it was an apparition. She was only an angel. Hopes were raised, dashed, and raised again, and we who weren't claimed would run into the woods crying and comforting each other until it was time for supper. When I was older, I returned to the nunnery to get more details and look for someone myself, but it was too late. Sister Teresa had passed away and was a candidate for beatification in Rome. I never found my mother, my grandmother, or anyone from my family.

"Please tell me, who am I? I am a lost child of sixty! My hands shake. I have nightmares and I cannot sleep. I smile at strangers but am overwhelmed by tragedy. I work on crossword puzzles all the time. Words are secret doorways, you know. Crossword puzzles are sometimes indecipherable and mysterious. They are a scramble of codes I can solve, but I cannot solve my own code. My wife and children are Catholic. I was born a Jew and also baptized in the church. I come to these conferences every year to find people who can understand me. Am I a ghost, a goblin, a devil? My head is buzzing with a swarm of demons."

There was nothing more for him to say, and the group was uncomfortably silent while the woman sitting next to him stroked his hand.

My mind spun. I was transfixed by the man's face. He was the age of my brother, five years younger than I, and from my home town. I looked carefully at his eyes and face but saw no resemblance to the one photograph I have of Janek. What about Babcia Hancia? Did he remember her name? I dared not ask any questions. My neck stiffened, and the hair on my arms stood up straight. I decided to leave the room and take a walk. The white down of the poplars whirled around me like a blizzard. Who is this Wojtek? Could Janek have been saved in the convent? Has he been looking for me? Is this man really the person in the only photograph I have of my little brother, or is it simply wild happenstance? Memories and impressions swirled like *puch* and clung like glue as I walked obsessively around the lake. I took deep breaths but wasn't able to resolve anything.

Wojtek and I closed the *kawiarnia* late that night. We spoke of our losses, bereavements, and unrequited love. We both needed to accept each other and explain our grief, and Wojtek needed to have his present and future somehow validated. We talked about our children and grandchildren. He cried a little, puffed on a cigarette, and philosophized. "You know , Susan, a man can survive three weeks without food, three days without water, but he cannot survive three hours without hope."

That night I dreamt of fires and death. I found it hard to breathe and woke up troubled and perspiring.

But then day followed night—and I finally understood that day always follows night. I left Poland determined to sustain the hope that kept Wojtek and me—all of us—going. Perhaps you cannot, as Thomas Wolfe said, go home again. But I knew that you could go back to your past and reclaim yourself again.

Flying home the next day, the outskirts of Warsaw looked beautiful. I felt relief in the silence and resolution. A pleasant breeze was moving the summer leaves, and the day looked like an impressionist painting as I began the hard work of exorcising my demons, reorienting myself to the present, my partner, my children and grandchildren, and closing the internalized space of childhood memories and Polish ghosts that haunt them.

Everything that lives and endures
For more than a day after we die
Is eternal.
We live in the eternity of others.
We are their eternity.

—*Yehuda Amichai,*

"Posthumous Fragments"

This book has been set in Hoefler's

Requiem, derived from a set of inscriptional

capitals   appearing in Ludovico Vicentino

degli Arrighi's 1523 writing manual, *Il Modo*

de Temparere le Penne.